HAUNTED MISSISSIPPI GULF COAST

HAUNTED MISSISSIPPI GULF COAST

BUD STEED

HAUNTED
America

Published by Haunted America
A Division of The History Press
Charleston, SC 29403
www.historypress.net

First published 2012

ISBN 978.1.5402.3180.2

Library of Congress CIP data applied for.

CONTENTS

DEDICATION AND ACKNOWLEDGEMENTS

This book is dedicated to my wife, Jennifer Lynn Steed, who has never, over the years that we have spent together, lost faith in me, even when I have lost faith in myself. She has always been my constant cheerleader, offering words of encouragement and a hug and a kiss in those moments when I doubted myself and my abilities and always patiently waiting while I chased after one dream or another. She is my rock, and I love her for it.

To my kids, David, Sean, Ciara Jo and Kerra Lynn, I thank you for your understanding and patience when I was too busy writing and researching to throw the baseball or football with you or to simply hang out and watch *Tinkerbell and the Great Fairy Rescue* movie with you (after about the fortieth time, I can effectively quote the good parts by heart). Watching you guys grow and become the fine young men and ladies that you are is truly gratifying and a testament to your mother's hard work at raising you correctly. It's not easy being my kids, but you manage it well, and I love you all more than life itself.

To my oldest daughter, Bobbi Jo, I miss you constantly, and not a day passes that I don't think of you or wonder what your life would have been like. Rest in peace, sweetie. We all love and miss you.

To my good friend David Harkins, who is also the founder and director of our paranormal investigation team, The Ozarks Paranormal Society, thanks for always having my back and for always being ready to help, even on short notice.

DEDICATION AND ACKNOWLEDGEMENTS

To my parents, Merlin Sr. and Rose Steed, I thank you for never giving up on me even though I gave you ample reasons to do so. Your encouragement, love and forgiveness over the years are greatly appreciated, and I can only hope that I end up being half the parent to my children that you two were to me; I love you guys.

I would like to acknowledge the help that I have received while researching and writing this book. Thanks to Dave Harkins for riding along on the trip to the coast for photos and video for this book and for my websites. Your help was much appreciated, brother. Also, thanks to Jennifer for helping proofread the rough draft, for keeping me on task and on schedule and for keeping the kids quiet and occupied so that I could write. Thanks to Will, Katie and everyone at The History Press for all your hard work in bringing this book and my previous one to life; I appreciate each and every one of you.

INTRODUCTION

THE MISSISSIPPI GULF COAST

The Mississippi Gulf Coast is an environment unlike any other in the United States, with warm moderate temperatures, clean sandy beaches, emerald green waters and an eclectic mix of cultures ranging from Vietnamese to Creole, all wrapped up in a good old-fashioned dose of southern hospitality. Friendly people, a huge tourist trade and plenty of activities ranging from sport fishing to boat cruises to casinos make this once quiet area a bustling economic and entertainment Mecca.

Once known as the "poor man's Riviera," vacation homes of some of the wealthy of New Orleans and, indeed, some of the wealthy of the South once dotted the coastline where casinos, condos and motels now stand. Canneries that once employed children as young as five years old as shrimp pickers and oyster shuckers are long since gone, replaced by warehouses and customs docks to service the huge seaports. Much has changed over the years, and the area has witnessed much tragedy to accompany the economic success that it has enjoyed. Two hurricanes—Camille in 1969 and Katrina in 2005, which destroyed nearly 90 percent of the buildings along the Gulf—caused tremendous damage and loss of life, but true to their Gulf Coast roots, the residents of the affected communities rallied together and started rebuilding their homes, businesses and lives in the aftermath of both tragedies. Toughness and resilience seem to be as much a part of Gulf Coasters' lives as the sea air that they breathe.

While the Gulf Coast of Mississippi has become a destination for those searching for entertainment and a chance to relax in the sunshine, it also harbors a darker side. When night descends on the beaches and the towns, when the neon lights of the casinos start to dim a little and shadows become more pronounced, a different side of the Gulf Coast starts to emerge. Strange stories of murderous sea captains, pirates and murdered slaves start to come to mind, as do tales of hauntings and ghosts. Nearly every community along the Mississippi Gulf Coast has at least one legend or ghostly tale to share; some have many. We will examine each city and town's local legends and stories of hauntings individually, starting at the western side of the Gulf Coast and moving east toward Pascagoula. To better understand why the Gulf Coast area is so haunted, one only needs to look to the history of the area.

THE HISTORY BEHIND IT ALL

Once home to the Biloxi and Pascagoula Indian tribes, the Mississippi Gulf Coast area had been inhabited by humans for centuries prior to the French settling in the area. Explored and claimed for France by LaSalle in 1682 and named Louisiana in honor of King Louis, the area claimed by LaSalle covered the Gulf outlet of the Mississippi and all of the land drained by it. Needless to say, this was a huge amount of land. With Spanish settlements slowly encroaching upon the land claimed by the French, King Louis XIV directed that a French presence should be established along the coast so that France might have a way to defend its territories from others who would attempt to claim them for their own. Enter one French explorer by the name of Pierre Le Moyne, Sieur d'Iberville, who, answering the call of his king set out to colonize the Gulf Coast area in the name of France. Landing at the deep-water anchorage off Ship Island, d'Iberville established a base camp from which explorations of the Gulf Coast were conducted to find a suitable location to establish a permanent settlement.

In April 1699, a settlement was established at the site of present-day Ocean Springs and named Fort Maurepas. It would be the significant site of French presence in the area until 1702, when it was decided by Jean Baptiste Le Moyne, Sieur de Bienville, to move the settlement to the Mobile Bay area. That lasted until about 1717, when a hurricane destroyed the harbor at Dauphine Island, culminating in the French moving back to Fort Maurepas around 1719.

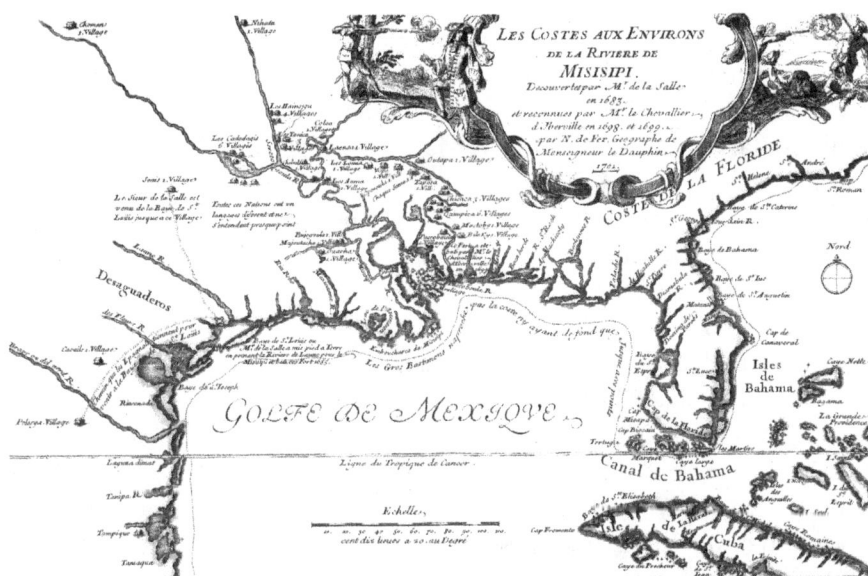

A map of the Gulf Coast created in 1701 by Nicolas De Fer. *Courtesy of the Library of Congress, call #G4042,M5,1701.84.*

In 1720, they moved yet again across the Biloxi Bay to establish Nouveau Biloxy (New Biloxi) near where the Biloxi Lighthouse stands today, with the old settlement of Fort Maurepas becoming known as Vieux Biloxy (Old Biloxi). The move occurred to provide easier access to Ship Island. Once again, in 1722, the French up and moved the capital of Louisiana to New Orleans, deciding that it presented a safer place from the possible hurricanes and tropical storms that threatened the area each year.

Fast-forward to 1763, when, as a result of France losing to England in the Seven Years' War (1756–63), all of the French holdings in the North American colonies, with the exception of New Orleans, became part of British West Florida. This also was short-lived, as Spain declared war on England in 1779 and Spanish-American forces led by Galvez and Pollock defeated the British at both Mobile and Pensacola in 1781. Defeated, the British under the Treaty of Paris in 1783 gave the British West Florida holdings to Spain, which managed to hold onto them until the Republic of West Florida was declared in 1810. During this time, pirates, or privateers, were running rampant throughout the Gulf Coast and the Caribbean. The three major players—France, England and Spain—all employed them in one form or another during their wars to expand their landholdings and to inflict damage on the opposition's merchant and naval fleets. During times

11

of peace, however, their legal charters to plunder were revoked, which really didn't mean a whole lot to some of the privateers, who then continued to plunder all sides, deciding that a life of piracy was a whole lot easier than fishing or farming for a living. A lot of famous pirates, such as Jean Lafitte and Black Caesar, sailed the Gulf using the barrier islands and natural secluded harbors as safe havens, places to lay low and hide their stolen treasures until it was safe to frequent the cities of the Caribbean and party their stolen money away on rum, fancy clothes and prostitutes. Stories of Lafitte hiding his treasure hoards and then murdering the crew members who helped him bury it are told all across the Gulf Coast from Mississippi to Texas. Phantom crew members have been reported on Ship Island, supposedly guarding Lafitte's gold to this day, and reports of ghostly ships, their masts at full sail, have been seen off the shores of the barrier islands. Perhaps they are explorers or maybe pirates still plying their bloody trade in the afterlife.

And so it went from explorers to settlers to privateers until the area came under the control of the United States in 1811, and Mississippi was admitted to the union in 1817. In the space of approximately 129 years, from 1682 to 1811, the area changed hands four times, from the Native Americans to the French, French to the British, British to the Spanish and Spanish to the Americans. During each of these exchanges, life continued to carry on, the influences of each culture playing some part in the formation of the Gulf Coast, as did the cultures that were brought to the area by American statehood. Each group of people brought its own stories, superstitions and beliefs along with it in its search for a new start along the coast.

In a short time, the cities along the coast grew, and the industries of timber, charcoal and fishing were soon the major suppliers of jobs and income to the ever-growing population of immigrants. A burgeoning tourist industry formed as well, with the Gulf Coast becoming a resort area for some of the more wealthy planters and businessmen, who built fine homes along the coast. Hotels and cottages were built to house those vacationers who were not as well-to-do or who were single but enjoyed visiting the Gulf Coast area as well.

The Civil War interrupted life briefly, but after the capture of Fort Massachusetts on Ship Island early in the war by Union forces, the area saw very little in the way of military action, other than an occasional skirmish or naval shelling. As with most coastal areas of the South, the tourist industry was decimated by the war, with families concentrating more on survival than vacationing, although people living along the coast did fare somewhat better than their inland counterparts due to the availability of fresh seafood.

Fort Massachusetts would become a prison to house captured Confederate soldiers and a base for the U.S. Second Regiment, known as the Louisiana Native Guards, which was one of the first African American combat units to actively fight in the war. Sightings of ghostly soldiers have been reported at Fort Massachusetts, perhaps still performing their duties of guarding prisoners or keeping watch for enemy vessels.

Life along the Mississippi Gulf Coast slowly returned to normal after the Civil War. The tourism and seafood industries employed large numbers of workers, as did the railroad. Toward the end of the nineteenth century and into the twentieth, canneries were established along the coast, with fish houses—little more than wooden shacks—being built to help process the day's catch. Children as young as five years old were employed at these canneries helping to sort and grade shrimp or shuck oysters. A boy of eight years old could earn twelve cents each day as a shrimp picker or oyster shucker, good money in the 1940s when child labor laws were nonexistent and the safety of workers was not a priority of the business owners. Accidents occurred that claimed the lives of workers, some of them children whose spirits are said to haunt the areas of the old fish houses to this day.

During World War II, the United States Army Air Forces built Keesler Field, known today as Keesler Air Force Base. The base was a major site for aircraft maintenance and for basic training of pilots. A crash boat facility was maintained at Ocean Springs to rescue any pilots who might crash on training flights out in the Gulf. The famous Tuskegee Airmen received their flight training at Keesler Field and flew training missions out over the Gulf. Naval vessels were built at the shipyards in Pascagoula and are still built there today; the industry supplies jobs for welders, electricians, laborers and suppliers of the raw materials required to manufacture the ships. As in any training mission or manufacturing job, accidents can happen. Ghosts are said to haunt various buildings at Keesler Air Force Base; some are not too happy about being there or with the fact that women are now active members of the Air Force. Ghostly workers are seen walking about the shipyards only to disappear when approached. One story was told of a spirit that entered the break room at a shipyard in Pascagoula, sat down, opened his 1950s-era lunch box, looked inside and faded away before the other employees' eyes. Needless to say, break time was immediately over, and everyone present vacated the break room without delay.

The entire Gulf area would, without a doubt, be unrecognizable to the explorers and settlers who set foot on the shore at Ocean Springs way back in 1699. The area continues to grow and prosper in spite of economic downturns and the stumbling blocks that Mother Nature continues to throw at it occasionally and will undoubtedly continue to do so; the future for the Mississippi Gulf Coast looks bright indeed. The future also looks bright for paranormal investigators in the Gulf Coast region; history and local tragedies have seen to that. Let's start our exploration of the haunted Mississippi Gulf Coast in one of my favorite coastal towns, Waveland.

CHAPTER 1
WAVELAND

The city of Waveland, as cities go, is actually pretty young, having been incorporated in 1972. The town of Waveland is much older than that, with established homes and businesses dating back to around 1800, or some say even earlier than that. The entire area from Waveland east to Biloxi was once the favorite vacation spot for the wealthy of New Orleans, a place to escape the stifling heat and humidity of summer for a chance to play in the emerald Gulf waters and relax in the cool sea breeze. As the expensive vacation homes were built along the coast at Waveland, businesses were established to provide the needed services that the wealthy demanded, and the village of Waveland sprang slowly into existence. Hotels were built to provide lodging for those not quite wealthy enough to build expensive homes and to service the single population that desired to vacation there as well.

The small village continued to grow and prosper, fueled by the tourism trade and the fledgling fishing industry. When the Civil War began, Waveland, like much of the Gulf Coast, saw very little in the way of military action. Like others in the South though, residents of Waveland did experience hardship, with food being in short supply at times. When corn and other staples were available, they were at inflated prices. The fishing and tourism industries rebounded after the Civil War, and the town grew steadily, becoming known as a nice, quiet place not only to visit but also to live. The wealthy continued to build and vacation not only there but all along the coast, and Waveland was the site of more than one grand party being thrown along the beach.

A beachside Victorian cottage in Waveland, January 1936. *Courtesy of the Library of Congress, call #LC-DIG-FSA-8c52054.*

All along the beach were mansions and fine Victorian homes with private piers jutting from the shore out into the Gulf. Unfortunately, very few of these homes remain; hurricanes such as Camille and Katrina destroyed an estimated 90 percent of the structures along the coast, and Waveland was hard hit by both of these hurricanes. Camille destroyed the historic Pirate House and numerous other homes, and what she didn't take, Katrina blasted ashore and destroyed. Libraries, historical societies and government buildings all along the coast fell to the destructive fury of Katrina as she scored a direct hit on Waveland as she came ashore. The devastation was extensive, with storm surges washing over Beach Boulevard and far inland into the city, washing away homes, businesses and the collected memorabilia and possessions that their residents were forced to leave behind. Not since Camille struck the coast in 1969 had Waveland witnessed such complete and utter destruction.

The city of Waveland has rebounded over the years since Katrina rammed ashore, but everywhere you look there are reminders of the devastation: empty lots with sidewalks leading up to where homes once stood; foundations sitting amidst a sea of weeds and tall grass, marked with "For Sale" signs. Some stalwart people have rebuilt, with new homes dotting Beach Boulevard and signs of more new construction underway. Sadly though, despite the ongoing commercial construction and people continuing to rebuild their homes and lives, so much of historical value was lost to both Camille and Katrina that the charming landscape of mansions and elegant Victorian homes has, for the most part, been lost to us forever. They can now be found only now in the black-and-white photographs housed at the Mississippi State Archives, the Library of Congress and in the private collections of individuals along the coast who managed to save them from the surging waters. One such home that withstood numerous tropical storms and hurricanes only to fall victim to Camille was the famous Pirate House.

THE PIRATE HOUSE

Thought to have been built around 1802 by a wealthy New Orleans businessman who was rumored by some to have been the leader of the pirates who sailed the waters off the Gulf Coast, the Pirate House was a beautiful home, strongly built to withstand the storms yet still elegant and large in its construction. The home was built in the Louisiana Planter style, with a brick-bottom floor and outside stairs that led up to the first floor. A large front porch ran the entire length of the home, with squared wooden columns supporting the gallery. White stucco walls, dormer windows and beautiful banisters of iron, much like what you would see on homes in New Orleans, made this home spacious and elegant.

The home sat at 649 North Beach Boulevard in Waveland and was well known to all who lived in the town or spent any time at all there. The home, also known locally as the Lobrano House, sat on a slight rise above the street and had a commanding view of the Gulf. It was also reported to have a secret tunnel that led from the home down to the water's edge. Workers reportedly discovered a section of the tunnel while working on building Beach Boulevard in the 1920s, though several sections of the tunnel were reputed to have been caved in between the road and the home itself. The construction of such a tunnel would have been difficult to accomplish but not impossible, as the area would have been fairly secluded at the time the home was built. The home was constructed next to a large pond and a bayou, which would have made it easier to carve the passage from the shoreline up to the property and

The site of the infamous Pirate House. When Hurricane Camille hit the coast, the home was completely destroyed. No one has ever rebuilt on the haunted spot. *Photo by the author.*

allowed small boats to enter the property unseen. It is thought, although it cannot be 100 percent confirmed, that the home was owned by none other than the famous pirate Jean Lafitte, who used the passage from the Gulf to the property to secretly smuggle contraband such as slaves, or "black ivory," as they were commonly referred to. While trafficking in slaves was legal in the United States, in 1808, Congress outlawed importation of slaves into Louisiana. President Thomas Jefferson, whose own ideals concerning slavery were muddled at best, appointed W.C.C. Claiborne as governor, a person whose known stance was definitely against slavery. So this all lends itself well to the possibility that the Pirate House was used as a place to disembark and hide slaves until such a time as they could be smuggled into Louisiana by way of the coastal waters and lakes surrounding New Orleans. The smuggling of contraband slaves would have been a lucrative endeavor, and one could hardly doubt that as bold and adventurous a man as Jean Lafitte would not have recognized it as such and had a hand in the smuggling operations.

All speculation aside, can Jean Lafitte actually be tied to the Pirate House, or is it all merely legend and yarn passed down from generation to generation? The name Lafitte can be found in a number of Hancock County records dating back to the early 1800s, as one Jean and Clarisse Lafitte owned a number of properties in the area, including the land close to the Pirate House and supposedly even the land that the Pirate House sat on. But was it actually *the* Jean Lafitte of swashbuckling pirate fame or simply someone sharing a common name? No one knows for sure, and we probably never will, but it does make an interesting basis for the stories associated with that particular property.

The home changed hands many times over the years, and with each successive transfer, stories were told about strange happenings and sightings connected with the property. Stories of specters and disembodied voices and sounds were told quite frequently by both the home's residents and guests. Several of the stories told are associated with a family by the name of Faulkner who supposedly resided at the Pirate House from the late 1920s to the early 1930s. Mrs. Faulkner apparently witnessed a ghost on the stairway several times and described him to friends and family as being a tall man dressed in rough clothing with an almost hypnotic stare that pierced through her with an almost violent force. He would stand at the head of the stairs for a moment and then vanish, never saying a word or moving, just staring his violent glare as if angry that she was in the home. Reportedly Mrs. Faulkner, an apparently stalwart woman who didn't scare easily, tried speaking to him and approaching him on several occasions but did not elicit any response.

Perhaps he was simply a residual spirit, an imprint of some past time in the life of the person, doomed to appear again and again like a bit of looped video film.

In addition to the spirit on the stairs, sounds of clanking, as of metal hitting metal, would emanate from the subbasement of the home, supposedly where the contraband slaves were secretly held. Sounds of moaning and cries would be heard from time to time coming from there as well, but when someone would muster up the courage to descend the stairs to investigate, no one would be found. Phantom smells rose up from the basement also, with the smell of tobacco being the most prevalent, along with a smell that was described as rotting flesh. Nothing was ever discovered that would account for these odors, even though they would reoccur occasionally, even after a good cleaning of the basement and lower floors. Another spirit, described as being only a shadow, was seen on occasion walking up the staircase from the basement area only to suddenly vanish near the top in what was described as a "breeze cold enough that you could see your breath in August."

One story that persisted for a while was that of three men who were stabbed and whose bodies were disposed of by dumping them down a deep well that was located on the property. The men were supposedly still alive when they were dumped into the well, and that would seem to be the basis behind the stories of faint cries for help being heard coming from the back of the property. In the evening hours when the sun had set and the light was fading quickly, the sounds of someone crying out for help could be heard. The cries were very faint, and it was once described "as if coming from the bottom of a well." Residents and friends—concerned, of course, that someone was hurt and needing assistance—searched the area repeatedly, and when they would come near the old well site, the cries would cease, only to start up again as the searchers moved away. This reportedly happened several times over the course of several years, always in the month of April. When the well site was eventually filled in, the cries for help never resumed; however, it didn't keep the specter of a dripping wet man from suddenly appearing near where the well was, staggering across the yard and suddenly disappearing. Multiple sightings occurred of a man dressed in what was described as "castoff ragged clothing" staggering from the back of the property, one hand clutched tightly to his abdomen as if in distress. He was reported to move slowly toward the back of the house only to collapse suddenly and fade from sight as he lay on the ground. The first time he appeared, Mr. Faulkner supposedly witnessed it from a back window. He immediately recognized that something was amiss with the man and rushed from the home to render assistance. As he ran through the open back door, to his amazement, the man collapsed and vanished before his eyes. Dumbfounded, he searched the immediate area but found nothing and so retired to the house to relate the story to Mrs. Faulkner. The man was sighted numerous times over a period of forty years by each subsequent owner of the property, all describing the same thing. After Hurricane Camille destroyed the home, no further sightings of the man were reported. Perhaps the ferocious winds and rain washed the residual spirit away. It didn't, however, erase the spirit of the wood chopper.

A story persisted from the late 1800s on about the sighting of a spirit chopping wood at the back of the property. This ghost, in his rolled-up shirtsleeves, was supposedly chopping wood as if to gather a bit of kindling for a cooking fire. He would go through the motions of chopping with the sound clearly heard, bend down as if to gather up the wood and then rise up and walk toward the house, only to fade away after a few steps. This sighting was infrequent, and no pattern could ever be established for it. One day he would be there, and then he might not be seen for months, only to reappear busting up some wood for a fire. After Camille ravaged the area, he was spotted a few times adhering to his set routine of chopping, a residual reminder of someone's daily chore. In the past few years his specter has not been seen, but the sounds of someone chopping wood, the thudding bite of an axe striking a log, has been heard, although with less and less frequency as time goes by. Perhaps this memory of a daily routine is slowly fading away and will one day be no more, just as the man wielding the axe ceased to be so many years ago.

BUCCANEER STATE PARK

A few miles to the west down Beach Boulevard lays the Buccaneer State Park. Like the rest of the coast, it was ravaged by Katrina. Every park facility was destroyed and washed away by the 140-mile-per-hour winds and the twenty-eight-foot tidal surge. It took years to finally get the park restored and opened back up, and even today, there are still various phases of construction going on. Thanks to all the hard work, today it is a wonderful state park with modern facilities, a wave pool, a water park, bathhouses and plenty of activities to keep both young and old occupied.

The area was in use for many years before it was designated as a state park. It was frequented by the pirates who operated in the coastal waters and, one would imagine, by Jean Lafitte himself, since the home he is attributed to owning is just a short way down the beach. The area of the park was also known as Jackson's Ridge due to the fact that Andrew Jackson established his base of operations there during the Battle of New Orleans. Jackson liked the area so much that he later returned and built a home on property that is now part of the park.

Several tales of ghosts and apparitions are attributed to the park areas, most notably one of a pirate seen rushing through the tall grass near the primitive camping area. He is reported to be seen moving along at a slow trot, cutlass in hand. He is, by all accounts, a rather tall man dressed in ragged and tattered clothing and seems to be looking for something in the grass as he moves along. He runs about thirty yards and then just fades away in a whitish haze that then just dissipates. It was reported that when a young man who was camping near the field saw him, he called out to him, and the pirate turned his head as if acknowledging that he heard him and then continued to fade away. The young man, unsure of what he had just witnessed, walked over to where he had seen the pirate trotting along but found no sign of anyone having been in the area at all.

The sound of boat oars in the water and the splashing of several men leaping from the boat as it grounded have been reported in the early hours of the morning and late in the evening. Soft murmuring and laughter accompany the sounds of orders being given and the thudding of the oars as they are placed in the boat and carried across the roadway to the campground. This story was told to me many years ago when I lived in D'Iberville, near Biloxi, by John, a local man who witnessed the phantom beach landing while walking the shoreline at night, although he is only one of several who have experienced nearly the same thing.

John was living in Waveland at the time of the occurrence and was a frequent sufferer of insomnia. It helped him to take slow walks along the beach at night; the sound of the waves washing ashore and the gentle breezes made it easier for him to relax. As he was slowly walking along the beach, he heard the sound of oars in the water carrying in the wind, and as he walked along, they got louder and louder. He thought that perhaps someone was out boating in the moonlight, and soon it sounded as if they were going to be landing right down from where he was walking. He heard the soft sound of hushed talking, and though he strained to see a boat on the water, there was nothing to be seen. All of a sudden he could see the imprint of a boat prow in the sand in front of him, and the tracks of feet suddenly appeared on each side of it. He froze in his tracks as he watched several sets of phantom footprints walk across the beach, accompanied by muted talking and laughter. The voices quieted as they got farther away from the imprint of the boat and then faded altogether. John snapped out of his frozen amazement and cautiously approached the imprint of the boat prow in the sand, not believing what he had just witnessed. As he got within a foot or two of the imprint, he said that it suddenly got very chilly, and goose bumps and hair began to rise on his arms and neck. Suddenly, as if it was whispered in his ear, he heard a voice say, "Move along, monsieur," at which point he spun around, startled to see who was behind him. Only no one was there at all. John said he whirled around and ran down the beach as fast as his legs would take him. That was the end of his moonlit walks along the beach for some time, as he preferred instead to walk along the well-lit streets. Perhaps he witnessed the landing of a group of phantom pirates up to no good in the moonlit night, smuggling contraband to or from the beach. Whatever it was, it was without a doubt intelligent, as it interacted with John by telling him to move along. It would seem that whatever they were up to, they wanted no witnesses to it.

One other sighting on the beach near Buccaneer State Park is that of a mysterious young woman who stands and watches the water. Said to be a young woman dressed in the fashion of the 1920s, she stands at the water's edge staring out over the waves. Those who have seen her say that she simply stands there as if in a trance, unable or unwilling to acknowledge those who have called out to her. After standing there for a few minutes, she suddenly darts out into the water and disappears. Thinking that she might be in distress, those who have witnessed her rush into the water run to her assistance, only to find that no one is there. No one knows who she is or why she stands there, let alone why she suddenly darts into the water, but my guess would be that perhaps the poor girl, waiting at the water's edge for her man to return, suddenly rushes out to meet him upon his arrival. I would much rather think that it had a happy ending than a tragic one.

CHAPTER 2
BAY SAINT LOUIS

B ay Saint Louis sits a few miles east of Waveland along Beach Boulevard and was discovered in 1699 by the French explorers D'Iberville and his brother Bienville, who named it Baye de St. Louis due to it being discovered on St. Louis' Day. Bienville visited the area several times, camping and hunting, before returning to their fort at the site of present-day Ocean Springs. Before departing, it was decided that about fifty men would remain behind, living off the land and with the friendly natives, and that they would begin the establishment of a colony near the mouth of the bay.

During the early 1700s, French ships would bring thousands of settlers to work the land grants being given to those who held favor with the king and court. One Madame de Mezieres received a grant of seventeen thousand acres from King Louis XIV that lay somewhat to the north of what is now Felicity Street in Bay St. Louis. Other large grants of land were given to a Madame Charlo and John and Philip Saucier, and the most important one of all on the shore of Bay St. Louis was given to a Thomas Shields, from which the first name of the city of Bay St. Louis, Shieldsborough, was derived. Two ships, *La Gironde* and *La Volage*, arrived at the bay on about January 3, 1721, and dropped off about thirty people destined for the de Mezieres grant. Arrivals such as these continued until France gave the area to the British after the French and Indian War ended in 1763. The land later ended up in Spanish control after the Revolutionary War wound down, and later, around 1812, the United States officially took control of the area, establishing the Mississippi Territory. Hancock County was formed

An image of the Bay Saint Louis shoreline taken in 1901. *Courtesy of the Library of Congress, call #LC-D4-105632.*

in 1812, and in 1817, Mississippi was granted statehood. In 1818, a charter of incorporation was filed for Shieldsborough, officially making it the oldest established city on the coast. While some of the neighboring outlying communities were developed to handle the harvesting and processing of the abundant pine and cypress forests, Shieldsborough quickly became a favored Mecca for both the wealthy of New Orleans and the planters of the Natchez area, with grand homes, hotels and establishments catering to the wealthy being built along the shoreline.

The city grew quickly and managed quite well for itself during the Civil War, other than the normal food shortages and black market price gouging usually associated with an area occupied by enemy troops. When the war subsided, the recovery was slow, but thanks to the Gulf location, the city rebounded quicker than the rest of the South, due in part to tourism and fishing. The ranks of the once wealthy planters and aristocrats had thinned considerably, replaced with northerners looking to profit from the reconstruction of the South. Known as carpetbaggers because their chosen form of luggage was made from used carpet, they came to the southern coast seeking to cash in on the availability of cheap land and to profit from the fact that money, which they had in good supply, was an extremely rare commodity along the coast, giving them the ability to wield great power over the economically poor southern areas. Homes once occupied by the southern elite passed slowly into new hands, and new businesses were established by both locals and newcomers alike. The usual mistrust of those who came to profit from the ashes of the defeated was to be found along the coast, just as it was throughout the South, but time has a way of healing most wounds, and these were no exception. Life in Shieldsborough soon found a rhythm of its own, as it did in other coastal communities, and the city flourished once again, enjoying good economic growth and stability.

All the new growth was not without tragedy though, as the city of Bay St. Louis—renamed by popular consensus in 1882—endured several notable fires that destroyed much of its economic center. The fire of 1894 destroyed much of the city square, leaving a number of people homeless and more than a few businesses completely destroyed. Another fire in 1907 destroyed the opera house and a number of businesses and homes, and a fire in 1927 broke out at Main and Beach Boulevard and destroyed six buildings. While the report of loss and damage was well documented for each of the significant fires, no report of injury or death from the flames was mentioned, so one could only hope that the occupants of the buildings destroyed in the flames made it to safety. But if some unfortunate souls did perish in the flames, that would account for some of the paranormal activity that was reported over the years.

Hurricanes Camille and Katrina extracted a huge toll on the coast in both property damage and loss of life, and Bay St. Louis was not an exception to their fury. When Camille ripped through the city, for three to four blocks inland the devastation was nearly complete, with only the odd section of wall or pipe protruding from the ground to mark the spot where homes and businesses once stood, a result of an estimated twenty-four- to thirty-foot storm surge. Lives were lost all along the Gulf Coast, with Bay St. Louis's neighbor across the bay, Pass Christian, suffering the most lives lost.

Katrina blasted into Bay St. Louis on August 29, 2005, destroying nearly 90 percent of all the structures within a half mile of the coast, with the storm surge traveling six miles inland in some areas and even crossing over Interstate 10. The bridge on Highway 90 from Bay St. Louis to Pass Christian was completely destroyed, as was much of Highway 90 itself, which was broken and washed away in some parts and covered with sand and debris in others. Many people lost their lives in this disaster; some people have never been found and are still counted among the missing today. Bay St. Louis has rebounded from this disaster, as it did from the previous ones, though even as of this writing, there is still plenty of evidence of the steady rebuilding and reclamation that has been going on for nearly seven years. Bay St. Louis, as well as the rest of the Mississippi Gulf Coast, has been forever changed by the natural disasters that tore it apart. But while the landscape may have changed, one thing has remained constant: the resolve of the coastal residents to pick up the pieces of their lives and carry on. It would seem that the resolve to stay, however, is not limited to the living.

CEDAR REST CEMETERY

Cedar Rest Cemetery, located on South Second Street in Bay St. Louis, is a very old place of rest, with graves dating back to 1820, when Bay St. Louis was still called Shieldsborough. A very well-kept cemetery, it is home to the remains of many residents of the bay area, both locally born and some transplants from as far away as Germany, France and Chile. All in all, over 2,417 souls call the Cedar Rest Cemetery home as of this writing, and at least one of them is a bit overprotective of it. I first heard this story while hanging out on the beach in Gulfport back in the 1980s from a guy who claimed to be one of a group of kids who witnessed it.

The story goes that in the 1970s, a small group of what could only be described as hippies used to hang out in the Cedar Rest Cemetery at night with the intent of doing a little partying. Pot was the apparent drug of choice for this group, and they had been in the cemetery for a short time smoking some weed and getting high when one of the group suddenly noticed that their number had increased by one, and he was not a particularly jovial sort of fellow. Kneeling on the ground slightly behind one of the kids was a man who was described as "a big guy with mutton chop sideburns, a scar that ran down the left side of his face and a stare that would make your blood turn to ice in your veins"—not the kind of companion they would have expected to appear in their group in the middle of a graveyard. Several of the group spoke to him, and an offering of the joint that was being passed around was made to him, but by all accounts, he just sat there and stared at them with an increasingly menacing look. One of the guys, either higher or braver than the others, ordered the guy to move along and leave them alone, but of course his request garnered no response from the kneeling man.

Emboldened, the guy reached out to grab the staring man to shove him away from the group—only to have his hand pass completely through him. That seemed to catch the kneeling man's attention, as it did the entire group, and suddenly the kneeling man wasn't kneeling anymore but was on his feet standing directly over the now terrified and confused young man. The rest of the group seemed frozen in place as the man with the mutton chop sideburns slowly bent down, seized the young man by the shoulders and lifted him completely off the ground. None of the frightened group of pot smokers, who suddenly didn't feel high at all, moved or said a word. When the young man who was being held suddenly kicked out with his legs, only to have them pass all the way through the man, it seemed to break the spell that the rest of the group was under. They tore out of the cemetery, leaving only the young man being held off the ground, a friend of his who was reluctant to abandon his partner to the unknown and the mutton chop sideburned ghost. As the story goes, the ghost leaned in very close to the young man he was holding onto, coming nearly nose to nose, and in a deep whisper told him that he didn't appreciate him being in his "house" and that he would be wise to leave and never return. With that said, he tossed the frightened young man to the ground, turned away, took several steps and simply faded away. Both young men ran from the graveyard as fast as their legs would carry them, most likely never to return. The validity of the story would of course be called into question simply from the fact that all participants—except the ghost—were high on pot, if it wasn't for the fact that the ghost of a man with big bushy sideburns has been spotted in the cemetery on several occasions since then. Whenever someone calls out to him or approaches him, he is reported to turn around, give the person a menacing stare and then disappear. Perhaps the group of partiers was hanging out on his tomb and he took exception to it, deciding that he should run them off and maybe hang around for a while to make sure no one else would bother the place, or maybe he just didn't like the looks of the potheads. Who knows? One thing is for sure though—I doubt that particular group ever slipped in to the cemetery to get high after that.

In addition to the ghost with the Elvis-style sideburns, sightings have been reported over the years of strange orbs of light darting among the tombstones and swirls of mist that would gather over graves just to fade as quickly as they formed. The specter of a young woman with a parasol has been seen on two separate occasions turning off the sidewalk into the graveyard only to disappear after a few feet, both times turning as if to acknowledge the individuals who have seen her and spoken to her.

The Cedar Rest Cemetery is, by day, an inviting and quiet place. As you walk among the tombs, the peacefulness of the place is hard to reconcile with the stories of the menacing spirit that protects it from those up to no good; however, if you visit in the evening, just as night is starting to fall, the place takes on a different sort of feel, one that makes you feel as if, maybe, you should just hurry on by and not look back.

THE HISTORIC TRAIN DEPOT

The Bay St. Louis Train Depot was originally a wooden Queen Anne–style building built in 1876 and served the traveling public until a fire completely destroyed it in 1926. From that point until 1928, when construction began on the new depot, Bay St. Louis was left without any type of permanent depot structure. The new depot, as it is seen today, was built in a Spanish Mission style and was opened to the public on April 20, 1929. The depot stayed busy bringing day-trippers from New Orleans to the coast during the Great Depression and served as a refueling stop for troop trains during the

The historic Bay Saint Louis train depot. It survived Hurricane Katrina and was used as the headquarters for emergency services during the cleanup. *Photo by the author.*

Second World War, when local vendors would sell food and refreshments to passengers through the doors and windows of the trains while they were stopped. In the 1960s, when passenger traffic through the station came to a halt, a movie starring Robert Redford and Natalie Wood was filmed there titled *This Property Is Condemned*, and it created quite a buzz for the community. Film crews, producers and all the accoutrements that go with making a movie flooded into Bay St. Louis, along with all the locals from across the coast who hoped to catch a glimpse of the stars.

After the movie, the station was reduced to servicing freight cars until the city eventually purchased the building and had it listed as a historic property and a Mississippi landmark. After a grant of $1 million for restoration and renovation, the depot was opened for public use as an event center. Hurricane Katrina caused some damage to the building, and it was used as the site of city government and health care services while cleanup and rebuilding were started. The building received a complete restoration after that and now houses the Hancock County Visitors Center and Tourism Bureau. It's a beautifully restored building, and it's easy to imagine how it must have looked to troops passing through on their way to ship out during World War II. Many a commuter paced the walkway by the tracks waiting for the train to arrive and whisk them away to work or leisure. A pleasant place to sit and wait, it was apparently so nice that one man decided to stay long after his earthly remains were gone.

As the story goes, a young man dressed in what is described as a white linen or "Palm Beach"–style suit has been seen on occasion strolling the walkway beside the train tracks, hands clasped behind his back and whistling what one person called "a merry little tune." It would seem as though he is waiting for the train because he stops every so often to check his pocket watch, only to resume his idle stroll up and down the boardwalk. This goes on for several moments until he makes a turn at the end of the walkway, tips his hat as if to some unseen person and then fades away. There would appear to be no pattern or reason to his appearance, as he is seen infrequently and at different times of the day and once even at night. As he seems to only interact with an unseen person, one would have to surmise that he is simply a residual spirit doomed to repeat the same thing time after time with no intelligent thought, sort of on continual replay. No one seems to know who he is or what circumstances trigger his infrequent visits, but all who have seen him agree about one thing in particular: he seems to be quite a nice, pleasant person who just likes to stroll the boardwalk.

CHAPTER 3
PASS CHRISTIAN

Pass Christian (pronounced locally as Pass Kris-chee-ANN) takes its name from a deep-water Gulf pass that was named for a local resident, Nicholas Christian L'Adnier, who lived on Cat Island around 1746. A son of early settler Christian de L'Adnier who arrived on the coast around 1719, Nicholas was the youngest of three sons. He married a young lady from New Orleans named Marianne Paquet, settled down on Cat Island and set about raising a brood of eleven children. The two channels in the Mississippi Sound were named for them both, Pass Christian and Pass Marianne.

The entire peninsula where Pass Christian is today was originally owned by Julia de la Brosse, otherwise referred to as the Widow Asmard. She had run a cattle and dairy farm managed by two overseers and some slaves since she acquired the land in the early 1740s. Some say that upon the widow's death, she left her entire holdings to her freed slave, Charles Asmar, who subsequently passed it down to his heirs. Others believe that it was procured through a Spanish land grant by a Spanish captain named Bartholemeu Pellerin sometime around 1809, when the widow passed away. He supposedly sold it to a Mr. Edward Livingston for the princely sum of $7,000 and moved with his family to New Orleans, basically due to the political turmoil that the area was experiencing. Which story is true I cannot honestly say, as I have never had the opportunity or time to delve into the property ownership records, but I would suppose that it really doesn't make a whole lot of difference in the end. A short two years later, a Captain Flood was tasked by Governor Claiborne with annexing the French settlers along

HAUNTED MISSISSIPPI GULF COAST

the Gulf into the Louisiana Territory as a sort of defense against the British. In January 1811, the flag of the United States was raised on the bluffs at Pass Christian. With the establishment of the state of Mississippi in 1817, more people started arriving in the area, and the settlement of Pass Christian slowly began to take shape. More of the wealthy established families started to acquire land along the coast. Homes were built for vacationing, and the 1830s saw the building of several fine hotels such as the Pass Christian, the Mansion House, the Sans Souci and the St. Nicholas House, which was for the exclusive use of single men who desired to vacation at the coast. In 1839, the first post office was built, and in 1848, Pass Christian was finally incorporated as a city. In 1849, the Southern Regatta Club was formed at the Pass Christian Hotel and was the precursor to the Pass Christian Yacht Club.

Growing alongside the tourism trade was the local shipping industry. Pass Christian was the site of many exports, including timber, charcoal and wool, shipping these items and more to markets all around the world. The shipping industry played a vital part in the growth of Pass Christian, but with the arrival of the Civil War, commerce in and around Pass Christian ground to a halt as people concentrated on survival. Only one conflict plagued the area, and that was the brief Battle of Pass Christian, if it could even really be called a battle. The Third Mississippi Regiment was stationed in Pass Christian, and upon word that an attack and landing was imminent by the Union soldiers at Biloxi, they quickly marched over there, leaving the town unguarded. The USS *Massachusetts* arrived on the scene and started shelling the town, trying to obliterate the docks and ships that were moored there. The shelling was brief and only stopped when a quick-thinking local woman dashed to her upper balcony and started waving a white bedsheet as a flag of surrender. The Union troops came ashore and plundered the town of anything that they could carry off before withdrawing back to their ship. The little one-sided battle became known as the Bedsheet Surrender, the only skirmish to occur at Pass Christian.

After the war, the railroad was built along the coast, and Pass Christian became more of a tourist spa and resort area than the center of commerce that it had been, with many luxurious homes springing up along the beach. Each new home grander and more opulent than the last seemed the order of the day as the wealthy tried to one-up one another. And so the city of Pass Christian grew, gaining in fame as a place for the rich to stay and play; it would keep that reputation for many years to come. An example of that fame was the Pine Hills Hotel and Golfing Lodge, built in 1926 at a cost of

$1,350,000 and furnished to the tune of a little over $200,000. It was the epitome of luxury and noted as *the* place to be; it even had five yachts on hand for the pleasure of its guests. Unfortunately, the timing in securing stockholders to build the grand resort was a bit off, and the Stock Market Crash of 1929 left its stockholders—as well as most of its wealthy clients— suddenly not so wealthy any longer. That resulted in the quick closing of the hotel and resort, a building that would go on to see many uses before finally being torn down.

The two world wars saw the residents of Pass Christian and all along the coast rush to defend liberty, both through military service and through drives for scrap metal, rubber and the other necessities required to manufacture and equip the machines of war. Many from the coast served bravely, with some making the ultimate sacrifice in the name of their country. After the wars, life picked up and moved on, and the city of Pass Christian experienced steady growth, with new businesses being established, as well as more luxurious homes being built, many in the form of apartment complexes where once stood some of the grand homes of the New Orleans wealthy.

When Hurricane Camille hit the coast in 1969, it caused almost total destruction of the city and the coastal homes. An apartment complex was destroyed, and a church was ravaged and thirteen members of one family were tragically killed, having left their home to seek safety in the house of worship. Overall, with seventy-eight lives lost, Pass Christian suffered worse than any other coastal community from Camille. Hurricane Katrina hit just as hard; of the almost eight thousand homes in Pass Christian, all but a mere five hundred were destroyed or severely damaged. The bridge crossing the bay to Bay St. Louis was destroyed, and for nearly a half mile inland from the beach everything was gone, completely leveled. Highway 90 or Beach Boulevard was fractured and broken, parts of it missing completely and other sections covered with sand and debris. Pass Christian was hit hard indeed, but with firm resolve, it has been rebuilt once more, although even today evidence of the destructive power of Katrina can be seen. Empty lots sit where once stood magnificent homes and businesses. Historic buildings are no more; foundations, sidewalks and steps leading to nowhere are still to be found, although with each passing month and year it's getting harder and harder to find them. While some people left Pass Christian, too broken in spirit to rebuild after suffering such a blow, others remained, determined to breathe life back into the community they loved. Some have no life of their own remaining, but they stay firmly entrenched in Pass Christian just the same, existing in spirit where once they lived in body.

PASS PACKING PLANT

The seafood industry has always played a vital part in every coastal community, and Pass Christian was no different. Residents have long enjoyed the bountiful harvest of local fish, shrimp and oysters plucked from the emerald waters of the Gulf. With the establishment of the fine homes of the wealthy, a demand for fresh seafood swelled, with the excess being packed and shipped by packing plants all along the coast. Situated on a little strip of ground on the bay, the Pass Packing Plant would process the day's catch, sending some to local shops and packing the remainder for shipment to New Orleans or other close-by cities. It took a lot of labor to man these plants, and quite frequently, children were pressed into service. It was not unusual to find children as young as five years old standing on overturned crates helping to sort shrimp or shuck oysters, working right alongside their parents. Child labor laws were disregarded, as were safety measures, and accidents were frequent—sometimes deadly.

The story of a ghostly shrimp picker was told at times back in the 1950s and 1960s and went a bit like this. People would be out enjoying the day, sitting along the shoreline simply relaxing, when they would become aware of a little boy standing there watching them. They would say hello, and the little boy would strike up a conversation with them. They always remarked at how oddly he was dressed, in old-fashioned, ill-fitting clothes, slightly dirty as little boys tend to get but always extremely polite and quiet. Inevitably, the conversation would turn to the "Where do you live? Where are your

The Pass Packing Plant, one of many seafood processing plants along the coast that utilized child labor, some as young as five years old. The photo was taken in 1911. *Courtesy of the Library of Congress, call #LC-DIG-NCIC-00867.*

parents?" kind of thing, to which the little boy would reply that he didn't live anywhere anymore and that he didn't have any parents. Well, people would naturally become concerned and ask him where he stayed, to which he would reply that he stayed at the packing plant. Most people found this odd since it wasn't in existence anymore. When pressed, all that he would say was that he worked at the packing plant. This would go on for a bit until the boy would suddenly stand up and start to leave. The witness would ask him where he was off to, but he would simply fade away before their eyes. It's interesting to note that he almost always appeared to women or elderly men, people with whom he obviously felt safe. Perhaps it was the ghost of a lonely little boy who worked at the packing plant and possibly perished in an accident or by foul play, or maybe he stemmed from some other tragedy that happened. No one knows for sure, and I think it's quite possible that we never will. It's kind of a sad story, though, to think of the little guy all alone like that.

PINE HILLS HOTEL AND GOLFING LODGE

Built in 1926 on land that was once the Shelly Plantation, the Pine Hills Hotel and Golfing Lodge sat at the north end of the Bay of St. Louis on approximately 1,900 acres and was a huge, 185-room building constructed at a cost of $1,350,000. Equipped with a large dining room with floor-to-ceiling windows, a separate dining area for children (aptly named the Jack and Jill Room), numerous terraces and sunrooms, lounges, an arcade, a tearoom and a sixty-four-car garage, the hotel was without a doubt the grandest one of its kind anywhere along the southern coast. The entire hotel was luxuriously furnished at a cost of about $200,000, with furnishings arriving by the hour to dress up the rooms finished on the bottom three floors while workers were still plastering the walls of the upper floors. The entire complex was built quickly and efficiently, with getting the hotel up and running the top priority, as the wealthy stockholders were anxious to stay and play in their new investment.

Unfortunately, the timing of building the magnificent hotel was just a little bit off, and a few short years after opening, it was forced to close its doors for good. The Stock Market Crash of 1929 suddenly left the wealthy stockholders and investors not so wealthy anymore. No one could afford to stay at the luxurious accommodations, and one by one the newly poor guests slipped away in the night. Several stories were told about guests who, learning of their financial ruin and feeling that their lives were suddenly worth nothing, cashed in their chips and checked out of the hotel and out of their lives. One man was found hanging by his neck, a rope tied through the transom window above the door from his room into the bathroom; kick marks marred the door frame where his hard-soled shoes kicked against it as he slowly choked to death against the ever-tightening grip of the rope. His specter was seen frequently in the room through the years, slowly swinging back and forth in the doorway.

The building was next occupied by the U.S. Army Engineers, with the 815th and the 818th Battalions arriving at the hotel in March 1942 and staying until 1946, when they were moved and later deactivated. From that point until 1953, it lay vacant and unused until it was reopened and converted into a seminary where priests of the Oblate Fathers, Our Lady of Snows Scholasticate, were trained and then sent out to do their work. They operated the seminary until Hurricane Camille swept ashore and caused considerable damage to the building, forcing it to be closed. In 1976, DuPont acquired the adjacent land to build its new complex, and in 1983, it bought the remaining land—about eighty acres—and had the old hotel destroyed, creating a natural buffer area between itself and the city. The area is now a natural area and is home to deer and other wildlife and is used by DuPont employees and others as a recreation park.

Many people who visited the hotel before it was destroyed commented on the seemingly abundant number of spirits who still called the old place home. Besides the hanging man mentioned previously, one story that was quite prevalent was that of the weeping woman in blue. As the story goes, visitors to the abandoned hotel reported hearing the quiet sobbing of a woman coming from one of the rooms adjacent to the lobby area. Upon investigation, they would find an older, dignified woman dressed in a beautiful blue gown standing in the middle of the room crying. She was said to turn and look at them as they entered the room with what could only be described as a look of absolute and utter heartbreak. Anyone who saw her would simply be rooted to the spot in disbelief, as no one was supposed to be in the building, let alone a beautifully dressed woman crying softly in the middle of a room. Reportedly she would look right at the person and utter one single word between sobs: "Why?" and then slowly shimmer and fade away, the sound of her crying still to be heard even though she was no longer visible. The question as to who she was has never been answered, and many possibilities exist. Could she be the spirit of someone whose husband committed suicide after the crash of 1929, or maybe one of the wives of the many stockholders or managers left broke and homeless? We will most likely never know. The destruction of the building didn't seem to move her on or put her spirit to rest. Several people have seen the vision of a woman in blue walking the trails and woods in the evening, crying softly as if in anguish, only to eventually fade from sight.

Another spirit said to be seen in the woods near where the old hotel stood is that of a man in the process of taking his life. Several times over the years, the man has been seen sitting on the ground with his back against a tree, a pistol in his hands. He, too, is said to be quietly sobbing as if suffering some huge tragic loss, the pain clearly evident on his face to those who have witnessed him. He slowly raises the gun to his head and, with his eyes tightly shut, pulls the trigger. Those who have seen him later remarked that they thought they were witnessing an actual live person committing suicide right in front of their eyes, complete with the sound of the gun going off and the bullet passing through his head with a spray of brain matter and gore. His body is reported to slump over onto the ground still clutching the pistol, his legs and body starting the drumming most associated with death throes as he slowly fades from sight. The shaken witnesses, once snapped out of their horrified trance, have all fled in terror, the sound of the gun still ringing in their ears, the vision of the body fading from sight firmly etched into their minds. Since Camille hit in 1969, I have only heard this story repeated once, and since Katrina not at all, so maybe the violent storms moved the poor retch on to his final rest. One could only hope that would be the case.

THE TRAGEDY OF THE RICHELIEU APARTMENTS

When Hurricane Camille blasted ashore, many people had evacuated to safety, while others chose to ride out the storm, believing that it would be no worse than other storms they had survived. They were, for the most part, sadly mistaken. One such group of people stayed in the upper floors of the Richelieu Apartments, believing that the building—designated as a civil defense air raid shelter—would provide them with a safe place to ride out the fury of the storm. Legend tells that twenty-three people stayed at the apartments and that only one person survived when the apartment building was completely destroyed. That is simply not the case, the result of a story told by one survivor who, at the time of the telling, might not have been aware that others had survived as well. The story took on a life of its own, with a made-for-TV movie about it even being made. The "lone" survivor, suddenly finding herself thrust into the limelight, started telling a story of a "hurricane party" gone wrong. Whether she simply was caught up in the excitement of her sudden fame or was a serial liar, no one knows for sure, but the story of the twenty-three people partying the night away in the face of a killer hurricane was simply a bald-faced lie. Others who survived the destruction of the apartment building came forward to set the record straight to try to stop the lie, but the media preferred the sensationalized account over truth, and it just kept getting bigger and bigger. Even today, the legend persists, much to the disgust of the survivors, many of whom lost close family members when the building was washed away. In reality, of the twenty-three people who stayed at the apartments, only eight were known to have died, the others enduring the fury of the storm clinging to tree limbs and debris after the building collapsed and washed away. They fought through the night to survive the violence of the storm, not knowing if friends and loved ones survived as well.

Today, no trace of the Richelieu Apartments remains, as the property has been redeveloped, but the legend still persists, even told by locals as being fact. The stories of witnesses passing by the vacant concrete slab where the apartments once stood and hearing the sounds of music and laughter as if a party were being held were told quite often in the 1970s and 1980s. I was first told the story in the early 1980s by a young woman from Pass Christian who swore that she had heard the ghostly party taking place. According to the storytellers, they would be passing by the slab at night when they would hear the sound of music and laughter coming from where the apartments once stood. Curious, they would move closer, and the music and laughter, the clinking of glasses, would get louder and more pronounced, only to suddenly be replaced by the sounds of glass breaking and screams, as if many people were dying. The sounds of the screaming would suddenly die away, the night becoming once more quiet and serene. Many people over the years claimed to have experienced this remnant from the past when Camille destroyed the apartment building, leaving only debris in her wake. Whether it was the product of overactive imaginations or they genuinely experienced something supernatural, it's hard to say, as many people lost their lives when Camille struck the coast. One thing is for certain though: the legend that sprang up around the Richelieu Apartments was based strictly in fantasy and—my opinion only, of course—for the sole gain of the woman who spun the original tale. This is a sad legacy to the eight people who lost their lives when Camille tore the Richelieu to pieces and a bitter reminder to the survivors of how the media loves a good story, true or not.

CHAPTER 4
LONG BEACH

The area that is today the city of Long Beach was settled by the French early in the 1700s, most specifically by the L'Adnier family. Nicholas L'Adnier, who had settled on Cat Island, petitioned the Spanish government in 1788 for a grant of land on the coast directly across from the island. He later moved to the land given him and built a home with rather large chimneys at Bear Bayou, giving most of Cat Island to his son-in-law, Juan Cuevas. After Nicholas passed away, the Spanish government gave most of the land that Long Beach sits on today to his widow, with the grant being known and recorded as the Widow Ladner claim. She later went on to give much of it to one of her sons.

The area grew in settlers and became known as "The Chimneys" after the L'Adnier home burned. Sometime around 1850, a man by the name of John J. McCaughan purchased part of the Widow Ladner claim and built a fine home that he named Rosalie. He had grand plans for the property and promptly ran an ad in the New Orleans paper trying to entice people to come to his fledgling settlement. He even built a one-thousand-foot pier out into the Gulf so that steamships could land to drop off potential settlers. The community was named Rosalie after his home, and it slowly grew and developed. Not much occurred there during the Civil War; no troop actions or camps are recorded. The fine homes that the neighboring cities to the west experienced didn't really develop here until after the war, the community being geared more toward commerce than relaxation.

When the railroad passed through the area, a resident named George Scott built the first train station, causing the community to be renamed Scotts Station. With the railroad passing through, commerce and industry picked up, and timber and salt were shipped out on a regular basis. A short while later, after pulling stumps from the land after harvesting the pine trees, it was discovered that the soil was perfect for the growing of certain crops, and a new era started for Scotts Station. Farming started to be one of the main sources of commerce for the area, and the little town continued to slowly grow and prosper.

By 1882, the heirs of McCaughan sold some of the land to the Thomas brothers, who started a fruit tree nursery. At about the same time, the town changed its name once more, this time to Long Beach. As more land was cleared from harvesting the pine forests, crops were planted, and it quickly became clear that radishes thrived in the soil. By 1905, Long Beach was incorporated, and by 1908, it had more than seventy individual growers and just over three hundred acres all planted in produce. Everything from lettuce to radishes to carrots grew well in the soil and produced bumper crops.

The city continued to thrive and prosper and, by 1913, had a population of about 1,200 citizens and even had a streetcar line that ran along the beach. In 1921, the farmers of Long Beach had an unusually large crop and shipped three hundred trainloads of their radishes north. The radishes, a long red variety, were a favorite in northern beer halls; the patrons would munch on the radishes while having a glass of beer or two. The land and farming boom unfortunately ground to halt when the stock market crashed in 1929, and eventually, some of the farmers lost their land during the Great Depression. The produce farming industry would never gain back the momentum that it had before the crash.

World War II saw members of the community taking up arms in defense of liberty and serving valiantly overseas, while other members of the community headed up the famous bond and recycling drives that were so prevalent during the war years. After the war, the city experienced a period of slow but steady growth. By 1980, it had grown to a population of about eight thousand.

Hurricane Camille hit Long Beach hard, destroying much of the coastal homes and businesses and killing about twenty-two people as it passed through. The devastation was great, but the city pulled itself back together, mainly from its sense of small-town community, where neighbor helps neighbor. The city today maintains that feel of small-town friendliness, even taking "The Friendly City" as its motto. With the exception of some terrible natural disasters, Long Beach has had a rather charmed existence, slowly growing with steady, hardworking people, avoiding the excess of the wealthy vacationers for the most part and maintaining its own identity. There were a few colorful characters that seemed to like the area so much they just couldn't bear to leave it—ever.

THE GHOST OF CAPTAIN PITCHER

Captain Cletus Pitcher was an English pirate/privateer who sailed the waters of the Gulf from the late 1700s to the very early 1800s. Thought to be part of the pirate ring led by Jean Lafitte, he plundered all up and down the coast, attacking any country's ship that he wasn't in a temporary alliance with and, truth be told, probably a few that he was. Pirates were notorious opportunists, and the good captain seemed to be cut from perfect pirate cloth.

He maintained a small treehouse, a shack basically built on stilts and wrapped around a tree, thought to provide a sturdier defense against the tropical storms and hurricanes that frequently hit the area. It was a safe place that he would retire to with his men to divvy up the loot and lick their wounds until the next pirating excursion or a party trip to the Caribbean. It was there, in his safe haven, as the story goes, that he met his demise. The captain had supposedly buried a large amount of treasure somewhere around what is now known as Pitcher's Point near the boundary of modern-day Long Beach and Pass Christian. The only problem with him hiding the stash of loot was that he did it *before* he split it with his men.

As you can imagine, that didn't sit too well with the pirate crew at all, so they confronted the captain about his greed and demanded to know where he had buried the loot. Captain Pitcher denied the deed, of course, but was unable to produce the accumulated treasure to satisfy the men. The arguing and drinking continued until it started to take a violent turn. Called a thieving dog by one of the crew, the captain leaped to his feet, pulled a pistol and promptly shot the fellow between the eyes. Left with an empty pistol and a now murderous crew, he retreated into his treehouse and barricaded himself inside. The crew, pretty hacked off by now, put a few shots into the house, to which the captain answered in kind. This back-and-forth shooting and name calling continued for a bit until one of the crew members had enough. He issued a warning to the captain to come out and surrender the treasure location or else they would burn him out. The captain reportedly answered the crew member by shooting him, which did nothing to calm down the situation. One of the crew threw a lit torch against one of the stilts that supported the house. The dry wood caught fire rapidly and spread up to the house itself, trapping the captain inside.

The crew, realizing that they were about to roast the only person who knew the location of the buried loot, tried to rescue the captain, but the flames spread too quickly, engulfing the entire structure in minutes. As Captain Pitcher met his demise in the roaring flames of his treehouse, it's reported that he cursed the entire lot, threatening to come back from the grave and have his revenge on them all. With that said, he reportedly laughed his way straight to hell amid the flames, his laugh ringing in the ears of the crew for some time after the flames had died out.

The story goes that the ghost of Captain Pitcher returned from the grave and personally saw to the execution of each of the offending crew members responsible for his death, seeking them out wherever they were and extracting his pound of flesh before moving on to the next one.

Several people have reported over the years seeing a large, bushy-bearded man dressed like a pirate walking down the beach, at times bursting into an almost maniacal laughter before disappearing. Those who have seen him face to face describe him as a man of middle age sporting a long, bushy beard covering a pockmarked face. They say that his eyes have a particular crazy look to them, which seems to scare the dickens out of whoever he is looking at.

Several times before development and such changed the lay of the land, those frequenting the point witnessed him charging across the ground at them with a look of indescribable fury on his face. The witnesses were so unnerved that they immediately turned tail and ran for their lives; however, when they recovered enough to glance over their shoulders, there was never anyone there. Perhaps they were getting too close to the captain's treasure hoard, the one whose location he took to the grave, and he felt that he must protect his stash. There's no way to tell, but I can say that if I witnessed the apparition of a maniacal pirate charging straight for me, I would probably turn tail and run myself.

THE MODEL T

One story that made the rounds from the 1950s through the 1980s was that of the phantom Model T Ford. Back when cars were just starting to appear in the coastal communities, a young, well-to-do man decided to purchase an older Model T. He dearly loved his "Tin Lizzie" and would spend hours puttering up roads that were really no more than wagon ruts in the sand. He had a habit of hanging out at the local eateries and general stores, bragging about how great his car was and flirting with the local ladies. This attracted the ire of some of the local boys who were not so well-to-do, good hardworking farm boys who looked at the wealthy young man as being a tad bit spoiled and obnoxious.

As the story goes, the young man enticed one of the local ladies, with whom one of the farm boys was secretly madly in love, to go for a ride in his car. She accepted and had such a wonderful time that she could talk of nothing else, which, as you might imagine, did nothing to soothe the feelings of our farm boy. Talking with his friends, it was decided that both the car and the well-to-do guy had to go. Long Beach just wasn't big enough for the both of them, and with the guy and his car out of the picture, the farm boy was sure that he could win back the affections of the young lady. A plan was hatched, and the wealthy young man received a note claiming to be from the young lady asking him to meet her near the beach when it got dark. It said that she was madly in love with him and simply had to see him and his magnificent motorcar again. Who knows what was going through the young man's mind as he puttered along in his car to the appointed place of meeting, but one could only imagine the anticipation that he was feeling. It's not hard to imagine his surprise when suddenly it's not the young lady who walks up out of the dark but, instead, half a dozen young men. To make a long story short, the wealthy young man stood by and watched helplessly as they destroyed his beloved car, tearing it to pieces in their anger. Unfortunately, they didn't stop at just the car. The poor young man was beaten to death, dumped into the remains of his car and unceremoniously dragged away by a horse team, to be disposed of in the bayou.

As the story goes, some say that on nights when the moon is dark, they can hear the sounds of a Model T puttering down Beach Boulevard in the early morning hours. Those who have seen him say that the ghost of a smiling handsome young man is at the wheel and has even tipped his hat in passing before fading slowly from sight a few yards farther down the road. Perhaps the young man loved driving the car so much that he just can't stop, even in death.

CHAPTER 5
GULFPORT

G ulfport was officially incorporated on July 28, 1898, although the planning and layout for the city started around 1887 with the land being surveyed and staked out. Two gentlemen are credited with the founding of Gulfport: William H. Hardy, who was president of the Gulf and Ship Island Railroad, and Joseph T. Jones, who later took control of the railroad and is credited with dredging the harbor in Gulfport, effectively opening up a channel to the sea and paving the way for the Port of Gulfport to be established. With the opening of the port, the lumber and turpentine that they were transporting from the small towns to the north that were serviced by their main rail lines and spur lines had a quick and easy way to be shipped worldwide. The town grew rapidly, with more businesses being opened to provide services to the many dockworkers and trainmen who brought in and shipped out the vast shipments of lumber and other commodities. From 1903 to 1907, more than one billion board feet of lumber was shipped out of Gulfport, transported to the coast by the Gulf and Ship Island Railroad. In 1910, a U.S. post office and customs house was built in Gulfport, aiding in establishing the security and growth of both the city and the port. In 1984, the Gulfport Post Office building was officially listed on the National Register of Historic Places.

Some fine homes were built along the coast, examples of how well the city's movers and shakers were doing financially, as well as a number of fine hotels, such as the Great Southern Hotel, constructed in part because Jones was in need of a southern residence once he had taken over complete control of

The main offices of the Gulf and Ship Island Railroad, 1910. The G&SI Railroad was instrumental in the building of Gulfport and the port itself. *Courtesy of the Library of Congress, call #LC-D4-34344.*

the railroad. The land to the east of the port developed into housing areas, with many fine homes such as Grasslawn being built close to the shoreline. A replica of the historic house, which was completely destroyed by Hurricane Katrina, was built using the original plans and to original specifications.

Gulfport was also the recipient of a Carnegie Library in 1916, the bill for the structure being footed by Andrew Carnegie of steel production fame. His Andrew Carnegie Corporation was responsible for building numerous libraries across the country, as his firm belief was that the knowledge gained through reading would serve a person well for the rest of his life and had contributed greatly to his success. The building housed the library up until 1966, when the library was moved into more modern and spacious facilities.

The city grew steadily and prospered greatly from commerce right up until World War II, when things slowed down economically, with the businesses and port focusing more on supplying the military than personal economic gain. Thousands of soldiers and navy men shipped out from the port and

The Naval Supply Yard at Gulfport, 1905. Most of the labor was done by hand with the aid of block and tackle. *Courtesy of the Library of Congress, call #LC-D4-34363.*

received specialized training in the area. The port was a major resupply hub for naval vessels, and in 1942, the navy put a Seabee detachment in Gulfport with the establishment of the Advanced Base Depot. Several schools were established to train guards and provide other skills. With the winding down of World War II, the base suffered cutbacks in both mission and personnel. Today, the Gulfport Seabee Center is the finest to be had in the world and an integral part of the Gulfport community, readily aiding its coastal neighbors whether in the face of disaster or helping to build a new playground.

Gulfport continued to grow over the years since World War II, annexing thirty-three square miles in 1993 and making it the second-largest city in Mississippi after Jackson, the state capital. According to a census done in 2010, the city of Gulfport boasted a population of 67,793, a pretty good comeback for a city that five years earlier had been almost washed away.

Like its neighbors, Biloxi and Bay St. Louis, Gulfport has embraced casino gambling within its city limits. The Island View Casino located on West Beach Boulevard has brought a lot of jobs and a huge economic boost to the city. The casino has all the slots and table games that you would expect and also has four restaurants and 563 deluxe rooms and suites. A nicely designed complex, it fits well with the area and is the only casino located in Gulfport, although Bay St. Louis has two and Biloxi has nine.

Gulfport is one of those cities that was founded on commerce and steadily stayed the course, developing the port facilities into some of the finest in the nation, locating numerous industrial areas throughout the city and helping small businesses flourish. Even though it has been partially destroyed by two major hurricanes in the space of thirty-six years, it keeps bouncing back better each time.

Tales of ghosts are as easy to come by in Gulfport as photos of hurricane damage, with stories being told about haunted houses, boating accidents turned fatal, fish house and cannery accidents and even the occasional murder victim looking for revenge.

GHOSTS OF THE PORT

The Port of Gulfport has been around since nearly the start of the city and is a huge employer of local Gulf Coast residents. Hundreds of ships load and unload their cargos at the port each quarter, coming and going to all parts of the world. In the early days of the port, loading and unloading was done with manual labor, men hoisting loads high with the aid of block and tackle or moving the loads by hand, rolling barrels from the docks onto flatcars or pallets to set into ships' holds. The work was hard and dangerous, and the occasional accident would happen, sometimes with fatal results. Several stories were told to me when I lived on the coast that stuck with me over the years, one in particular that the storyteller swore was true because he had experienced it himself, although everyone he related it to thought he was crazy.

David was in his mid-thirties when I first met him in Biloxi. We both frequented the same bar and, as acquaintances are apt to do, struck up conversations whenever we ran across each other. I got to know him fairly well and found him to be a pretty decent guy whom, although he liked to have a drink or two, I never saw drunk. He always seemed to maintain control of himself and never looked for trouble; he was just a decent guy having a drink. That's why his story stuck with me, I guess; he just seemed to be the type who would never fabricate a story, especially one of this type.

He worked at the Port of Gulfport and was in the maintenance department, fixing all kinds of things like the overhead cranes and forklifts. He was very

A view of the modern Port of Gulfport, a secure port facility that ships billions of dollars' worth of cargo overseas each year. *Photo by the author.*

mechanically inclined, and whenever something would break down, he was the one who everyone hoped would be sent to repair it. He was quick, efficient and really knew his job. He was also a bit of a risk taker at times.

One day, he was called out in the early morning hours to fix a crane that had broken down in the unloading of freight from a ship. A large crane that shot up extremely high into the air and was mounted on a permanent base, it had an arm that would swivel and extend out over the ships. He had to climb a ladder to get to the operator's compartment, and a catwalk extended along the top of the crane arm, allowing maintenance people to access the cables and pulleys at the end of the arm. The cables had stopped moving while being lowered back down to the ship to pick up another container or whatever it happened to be that they were unloading. David climbed up to the operator's compartment, performed what checks he could there and determined that he would have to climb out onto the catwalk and inspect the cables to see if he might find the problem. Safety is always important, especially when you are that high in the air and have to climb out on a catwalk that's swaying gently back and forth. David, realizing that he didn't have a safety harness, decided that he would just go ahead and go out anyway. He would just be extra careful and save the time that it would take him to climb back down to get a harness. The operator saw this as a perfect time to climb down and take a quick break, so that left David by himself on a catwalk high above a ship with no safety gear—not a good thing at all. He started out along the catwalk and got about three-quarters of the way to the end when the wind started to pick up a bit, causing the crane arm to sway much more than David was expecting. Before he even realized what had happened, he lost his balance and started to teeter over the edge of the safety cable. Unable to check his fall, he reached out and managed to grab one of the safety cables as he went over the edge. So there he hung by one hand high up in the air with no safety harness and no one around who could arrive in time to save him—or so he thought. Just as his grip was starting to slip and he thought he was about to die, he felt someone grab his wrist tightly, and he looked up to see a man—a stranger—holding onto his wrist with one hand and the safety cable with the other. Well, of course, David was hollering for help at the top of his lungs and pleading with the guy not to drop him, but the man never said a word, just smiled at David and firmly gripped his wrist. David said that the man lifted him up and helped him back onto the catwalk, where David lay on his back trembling at the close call. He looked up at his savior and thanked him repeatedly for saving him, but the man simply smiled at him and nodded his head. David closed his eyes for a moment, saying a silent prayer of thanks, and upon hearing several co-workers clambering across the crane arm to him, he opened his eyes to find the man gone. When he asked his co-workers where the man who had pulled him to safety had gone, they all looked at him and said, "What man? There was no one here but you."

Well, David knew that someone had pulled him to safety; he could see the man's face in his mind as clear as could be. Shaken and now slightly confused, he was helped back down to the ground, and after a good butt chewing by his supervisor, he was sent home for the remainder of his shift to pull himself together. As he was clocking out, he happened to glance at one of the photos from the 1950s that was hanging on the wall. It showed a group of men standing on the dock, the kind of image taken of co-workers to commemorate some special time or event. What he saw shocked him completely, for in the front row of the photo was the very man who had pulled him to safety. The photo was hung in memory of several of the guys in it who had died in an accident while working at the facility. Some type of fire that swept through the area where they were working had been the cause of their demise, and one of the killed was the man who had saved him.

Completely wigged out now, he rushed out of the facility and straight home, where he said that he immediately "poured himself into a bottle for three days," obviously trying to make sense of what had happened and assuring himself that he wasn't crazy. To this very day, David firmly believes that the ghost of the worker killed in the 1950s fire was his savior on the crane arm, and he tells the story with such conviction and emotion that one finds it hard not to believe him. Perhaps the worker, unable to save himself so long ago, saw the opportunity to save another and took it. Whatever might be the case, from that point forward, David stopped being a risk taker and followed the rules. He also made it a point to find the man's grave, and each year on his birthday, he leaves a small bunch of flowers on the headstone, a small thank-you to the man he knows gave him his life back.

Another spirit that is said to haunt the port is that of "the walker," who, when seen, always seems to be rushing off to someplace, walking along at a quick pace. He has been seen in just about every corner of the huge port at one time or another and is always described as a man in "really old" work clothes wearing a floppy brimmed hat and, curiously enough, in need of a shave. It's never been said that he interacts with anyone or even acknowledges anyone as close by. He just hurries on along his way and, after a few yards, fades away to nothing.

GRASSLAWN

Grasslawn was a beautiful home located on East Beach Boulevard in Gulfport and was built as a summer home for Dr. Hiram A. Roberts in 1836. Dr. Roberts was a surgeon from Port Gibson who also owned and operated several sugar plantations in Louisiana. Grasslawn was a beautifully crafted home of pine and cypress with ten-foot-wide porches supported by two-story columns. It contained three twenty-foot-square rooms on each floor, with the east rooms containing black marble mantels and the west rooms containing white marble mantels, all styled identically.

When it was originally built, it sat on 235 acres of gardens and orchards that were meticulously maintained and landscaped. The property was subdivided in 1905, and Grasslawn was purchased by John Kennedy Milner and remained in the Milner family until it was purchased by the City of Gulfport in 1973. Placed on the National Register of Historic Places in

Grasslawn Mansion, 1933. The home was completely destroyed by Hurricane Katrina, but the City of Gulfport completely rebuilt it to exact specifications from the original plans. *Courtesy of the Library of Congress, call #HABS MISS,24-GUPO,1-1.*

1972, it has long been a beloved piece of Gulfport history and is even seen in the lower left corner of the official seal of the City of Gulfport.

It was a favorite place for couples to wed, and numerous people started off their lives together with a loving "I do" said on the grounds of Grasslawn. Unfortunately, Hurricane Katrina completely destroyed the historic home, washing away most of it and leaving debris strewn across the once meticulously cared-for lawns. The City of Gulfport was not about to let its beloved Grasslawn fade away into memory, however, and plans to rebuild the magnificent home as an exact replica from the original plans maintained by the city were devised and carried out. Today, you can visit a replica of Grasslawn as it looked before the hurricane, the grounds slowly being cultivated back to their original glory. Once more, couples will be able to say "I do" in the beautiful gardens, having a dream wedding to remember, southern style.

For many years, reports of spirits being in and around Grasslawn were told, but none of them was frightening or vengeful. For the most part, they seemed happy to still be in the home and walking the gardens and didn't seem bothered at all to be sharing the place with the living. Several times the apparition of a man in early twentieth-century garb has been seen standing or walking the upper gallery, hands clasped behind his back. People who have seen him thought he was part of some reenactment that was going on, only to find out that there was no reenactment. He has been seen inside the home as well and even held the door for one elderly lady, nodding politely as she entered and smiled at him. His reflection has been caught in more than one photograph over the years, standing looking out of the upper-floor windows. His spirit has been seen walking the grounds in the evening as well, seemingly engaged in nothing more than a quiet evening stroll around the gardens. He always fades quickly away when approached though, perhaps preferring the quiet solitude of his stroll to an engaging conversation with a stranger.

A lady in a short dress reminiscent of a miniskirt popular in the late 1960s and early 1970s has been seen walking around the back of the property. She, like the man who is seen, seems to be in no hurry, just enjoying her walk, but unlike him, she has been reported to smile and even wave at people before suddenly disappearing in the wink of an eye. Those who have seen her remark on her exceptional beauty and nearly white blonde hair, saying that she has a dazzling smile that lights up her entire face. No one seems to know exactly who she is or why she has been seen at Grasslawn. Perhaps she was once wed there and fell in love with the place, as so many do, and decides to come back to visit from time to time. I would guess that would be as good an explanation as any.

THE GHOST OF MAGNOLIA DRIVE

A small family cemetery located off Magnolia Drive has been the scene of several unusual sightings. The Humphries Fowler Taylor Cemetery is a small, privately owned place of rest, so please, if you happen to be in the area and want to see if you can spot any paranormal activity, make sure that you have permission before entering the property; show the required respect not only to the dead but to the living custodians as well. Approximately twenty-two souls call the cemetery home, with the earliest burial date recorded as 1845 and the latest as 1955.

In a story reminiscent of "Resurrection Mary" of Chicago fame, a young lady dressed in clothing that some say looks as if it came from the late 1800s has been seen in the very early morning hours walking along Magnolia Drive. She is seen walking along the side of the road, moving along slowly and with a limp. Several people have stopped and offered her a ride, and each time she merely leans over and looks into the vehicle, straightens back up and limps along, never saying a word. Twice, though, she has accepted rides, and in both cases she has turned out to be quite a chatterbox. Both times she has been picked up by women; perhaps she just feels safer with them, or maybe protocol from whatever time period she might be from dictated that she not be alone with men. Each time she has gotten into the vehicle, when asked her name, she replies that it's Agnes and that she lives just "up the road a piece." They slowly drive away, and she starts in on this bizarre story of how she was out visiting her relatives and thought that her horse had thrown a shoe. She stopped the buggy and got down to check, only to have the horse take off running and the buggy wheel run over her foot. (That would explain the limping, I would guess.) She goes on to say how her father will take the buggy whip to that horse when it gets home and how she hopes she gets home first before they have to come looking for her, and on and on, all along the same lines. By this time, the poor woman who has offered the ride is no doubt thinking, "What kind of a nut case is this?" The young woman suddenly becomes pretty agitated and wants to be let out of the car, and I can imagine that the driver is only too happy to oblige at this point. She exits the vehicle at the cemetery entrance, turns to wave goodbye to the driver and then just fades away, leaving a shocked and somewhat terrified driver sitting there—although I doubt that she sits there for long.

As a side note, I looked up the listing of who was buried at this particular cemetery and found no mention of anyone named Agnes, so it may have been told to me wrong. All the graves are marked, so I have no idea about her identity. I can only say that if you are driving along Magnolia Drive and see a young woman limping down the road, you might want to think twice about stopping to offer her a ride.

CHAPTER 6
BILOXI

N ext to Ocean Springs, Biloxi is the oldest settlement on the Mississippi Gulf Coast and has a history of European settlement starting from approximately 1720, when the French settlement was moved back to the area of modern-day Ocean Springs from the Mobile area. Several months later, it was decided to move the settlement across the bay to near where the Biloxi Lighthouse stands today. A short three years later, it was moved again, this time to New Orleans, leaving only a few French settlers and their families in Biloxi. Life there didn't change much while France, Spain and England were trading it back and forth; there were just a few more settlers moving in here and there. It wasn't until the United States took possession of the area and it became part of the state of Mississippi that it really began to grow. Like some of its neighbors to the west, Biloxi developed into a summer resort area for New Orleans wealthy and for wealthy plantation owners from the Natchez area.

Grand homes were built all along the shoreline, and hotels and rental homes were built to service those who were either not wealthy enough to build the grand homes or who were single and just passing through. Vacationers flocked to Biloxi to take advantage of the cool ocean breezes in the summer and the variety of recreation alternatives available to them. Fishing, boating and grand parties became the norm during the vacation months, with life slowing a bit in the winter, as the locals took that time to do a little relaxing of their own.

In 1848, the Biloxi Lighthouse was built. It has since become one of the most photographed objects in the southern states. Manufactured in

The Biloxi Lighthouse, 1901. It has survived every hurricane since it was built with only minor damage and was built to help local fishermen find their way safely home. *Courtesy of the Library of Congress, call #LC-DIG-PPMSCA-18159.*

Baltimore, Maryland, and shipped to Biloxi, it has weathered every hurricane that Mother Nature has thrown at it with minimal damage. The light was a welcome addition to the coast, beckoning sailors and fishermen home to the welcoming shores of Biloxi.

When the Civil War broke out, tourism in Biloxi, like that of its neighbors to the west, dried up to nothing. After the Union forces captured Ship Island, it wasn't very long until Biloxi found itself occupied by Union troops. Some of the fine homes were commandeered for occupying soldiers and sailors of the Union forces. Biloxi was lucky in that it received no real damage from the Federal occupation or the war. Food was in short supply, and what was to be had was outrageously priced and came, for the most part, from the black market. As always, fresh seafood was a staple of the coast and was easily had.

After the close of the Civil War, life slowly resumed its leisurely pace, although carpetbaggers and everything associated with the Reconstruction period plagued Biloxi as it did the whole South. Properties traded hands, with the rich northerners buying up all they could pry away from the

View of the Back Bay of Biloxi, 2012. *Photo by the author.*

economically strapped locals. But eventually, life settled back down, and the tourism industry that was huge before the war regained its momentum, with the wealthy once again vacationing along the Biloxi shores.

In 1881, the first of many canneries was opened in Biloxi to take advantage of the abundant seafood of the Gulf. The Lopez, Elmer Company seafood plant opened on the Back Bay of Biloxi off Reynoir Street and canned both shrimp and oysters, as well as offered fresh oysters in bulk. As the seafood industries grew and more canneries were opened, Biloxi's population surged from about 1,500 people when the first plant opened in 1881 to about 3,000 people by 1890, the result of itinerant workers being brought in from Baltimore to work in the packing plants. Whole families, from the oldest to the youngest, worked in these canneries, sorting shrimp and shucking oysters.

During World War II, the United States Army Air Forces established Keesler Field as a major training site for aviators and mechanics. Many training flights were flown from Keesler out over the Gulf, and many pilots received their training at that base before being shipped overseas. The field became Keesler Air Force Base and is still an active training and repair base, having trained airmen for service in Korea, Vietnam and the Gulf wars.

After the war, Biloxi once again came to the forefront as a vacation spot, emerging as an alternative to Florida. In the 1960s, hotels were upgraded and chefs were brought in from Europe to try to provide the best seafood cuisine in the nation. When casino gambling became legal in Mississippi, Biloxi underwent a few changes again as large casinos flooded into the coast, building huge hotels and opening five-star restaurants. Billions of dollars have been brought into the coast as a result of gaming, and as of now, Biloxi's economy resembles a three-legged stool made up of casino gaming, tourism and seafood. All are experiencing great growth, and neither hurricanes nor oil spills can seem to put a damper on Biloxi's overall economy.

Biloxi is a great city, safe, with good schools and plenty of recreation options. Those who visit never want to leave, and those who live here can't imagine living anywhere else. That sentiment seems to extend beyond the living to those departed souls; it would seem that they may have departed their earthly bodies but not Biloxi.

BEAUVOIR

Once the last home of Confederate president Jefferson Davis, Beauvoir is now a memorial and historic shrine to the only president of the Confederate States of America. Its grounds are home to a large cemetery that houses the remains of 780 Confederate soldiers and their wives. In addition, a new presidential library is being rebuilt to replace the one destroyed by Katrina, where one can go to learn a little bit more about President Jefferson, the Confederacy and life in those trying times.

Beauvoir was finished in 1852 and was the summer home of wealthy planter and businessman James Brown. It was really a small complex, more than a summer home, and contained not only the main home but also two pavilions, a kitchen, a carpenter's shop and residence, the foreman's house, maids' quarters, chicken coops and a barn. Rounding out the complex was a carriage house and a harness shop. Very nearly a self-sufficient village of its own, it sat, at that time, about five miles west of Biloxi and four and a half miles east of Handsboro. To get to the Browns' home, you could either access it from the water by steamer or by way of Pass Road, which was a bit to the north. At the outbreak of the Civil War, the Browns packed up and moved north. The property was sold by court auction in 1873, approximately seven years after Mr. Brown's death. The new owner, Frank Johnston, hung on to the property for about two months before selling out to Sarah Dorsey, who named her new home

Beauvoir, the last home of Confederate president Jefferson Davis. This image was taken in 1933 while it was still being operated as the Jefferson Davis Soldiers' Home. *Courtesy of the Library of Congress, call #HABS MISS,24-BILX,V,1-3.*

Beauvoir (pronounced Bov-wah), which means "beautiful view," because of the lovely view of the Gulf waters.

Jefferson Davis, who had visited the home twice in the mid-1870s, fell in love with the surrounding natural beauty and peacefulness, and when the offer was extended to him by Ms. Dorsey to write his memoirs there, he readily accepted, moving to Beauvoir in 1877. He was joined at Beauvoir by his wife, Varina, in 1878 after her return from Europe and made arrangements with Ms. Dorsey to purchase Beauvoir for the sum of $5,500, to be paid in two installments. President Davis made the first installment, but before he could pay in full, Ms. Dorsey passed away. In her kindness, she left Beauvoir to President Davis in her will, making him sole owner of the property.

Davis passed away on December 6, 1889, and his wife and daughter, unable to care for the property on their meager income, placed a caretaker in charge and moved to New York City, even though they maintained possession of the property until 1903. It was then purchased by the Mississippi Division, United Sons of Confederate Veterans, under the clause that it be used as a home for Confederate veterans and their wives, as well as a memorial to Jefferson Davis

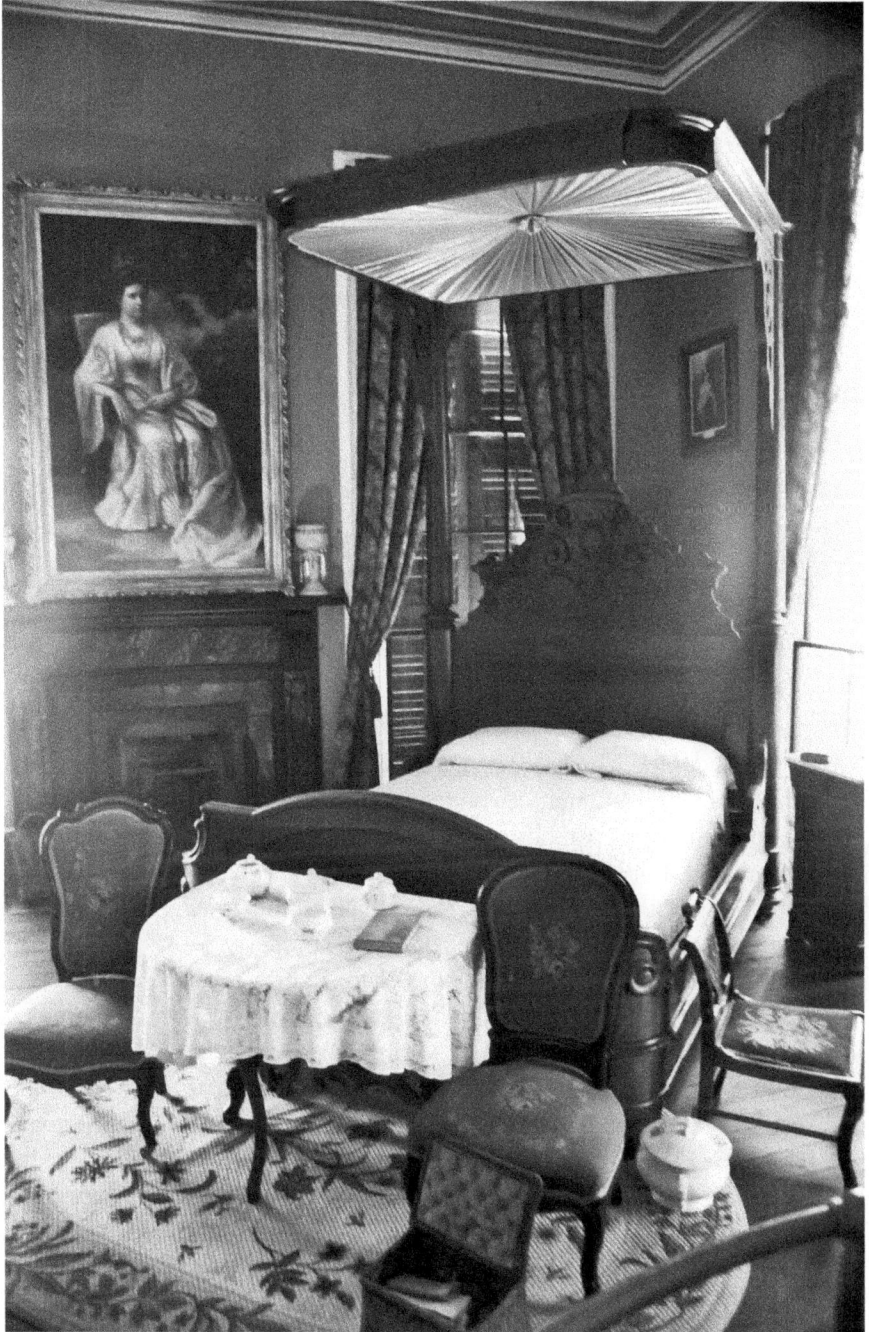

Winnie's bedroom at Beauvoir. She was Jefferson Davis's youngest daughter and never married. If the image is enlarged, a face can be seen in the shuttered window, even though no one is allowed in the room. *Photo by the author.*

The restored Beauvoir, 2012. Hurricane Katrina did severe damage to the home and grounds. *Photo by the author.*

and the Confederacy. The Jefferson Davis Soldiers Home opened in 1903, and soon, due to the growing number of residents, additional quarters in the form of a dozen dormitories, two hospitals, a dining area, a chapel and several other support buildings were necessary. In the fifty-four years that it was in operation, it served about 1,800 persons, with almost half of those being buried in the Confederate Cemetery located at the back of the property.

Today, this historic site sits on about fifty-one acres of the original estate and has been restored once more since Katrina caused massive damage. When Dave Harkins and I visited in April 2012 for the purpose of research and photos, the presidential library was still under construction, and the grounds and cemetery were still being landscaped and restored. The main home and the two smaller quarters had been completely restored back to their original glory, even down to the hand-painted faux wood patterns on the doors. It's a wonderful place to visit, with several rocking chairs for visitors to use lining the front porch area, allowing tourists to sit and experience the beautiful view from which the estate derived its name. It's peaceful and relaxing sitting there on the porch with the breeze from the Gulf washing over you. It's easy to see why Jefferson Davis and his family loved the home so much—so much that some say he never left it.

Before Katrina destroyed the gardens, part of the tour was a self-guided walking tour around the grounds. Jefferson Davis was a man who enjoyed gardening and raising fruit trees, so great care was taken by him in building and maintaining his gardens. That care was continued by the groundskeepers who maintained the modern-day complex with pathways around beautiful growing beds. Apparently, President Davis approved of their gardening, as several people have reported seeing the president strolling idly around the grounds, enjoying the beautiful flowers. They have remarked how much the "reenactor" looked like the photos of Jefferson Davis and how well he fit into the historical theme of the place. The employees and volunteers would, of course, be confused at what the person was saying, knowing that no one was portraying Jefferson Davis on the grounds. The official stance was, like at other historical sites, that there were no such thing as ghosts and certainly none on the property. That stance was put in question when a patron came to the gift shop and complained about the rudeness of the reenactor who was portraying President Davis. She said that she had stepped briefly from the path into the flower beds to get a better angle for a photo, stressing that she was careful not to have damaged any of the flowers. She stated that almost out of nowhere the person portraying Davis had appeared and basically read her the riot act for stepping into "his" flower bed, insisting that she leave at once. The employees apologized, of course, but reminded the woman that she *was* in the wrong for stepping into the flower bed to begin with. The disgruntled woman left, complaining loudly to anyone who would listen about the poor treatment she had received, vowing never to return, which I would imagine that no one who was present would have lost any sleep over.

President Davis has also been spotted sitting on the bench under a huge old oak with massive flowing limbs that nearly touch the ground in spots. This was reportedly his favorite place to sit while alive. In his later years, it was said that he would often sit on the bench and read, enjoying the solitude of the spot.

Dave Harkins, founder and director of our paranormal team, The Ozarks Paranormal Society, accompanied me on my trip to the Gulf Coast, and together we toured Beauvoir. We both took a ton of photos from both inside and outside the main home. Upon review, we found several anomalies present in the photos. In an image of the bedroom of Davis's youngest daughter, Winnie, we found a face in the window that has the shutters closed. After trying to debunk the image, we were forced to admit that there was the image in the window of someone who shouldn't

This massive oak tree stands in the yard at Beauvoir and is very old. Jefferson Davis is reported to have sat on the bench under its branches to read. *Photo by the author.*

have been there. The feeling that I got when looking at the image was one of sadness, as if the person was just deeply sad about something or other. Dave and I both felt as if we were being watched while inside and outside the main home and felt drawn to both of the daughters' bedrooms for some reason. When we were getting ready to leave, we walked up and asked the guard at the gate if anyone had ever experienced anything paranormal on the property. The official stance, of course, was no, but as we talked, we made mention of feeling something in the bedrooms, to which he replied, "You mean the two bedrooms on this side [east] of the house, don't you." He said this more as a statement than a question. We replied yes, and he simply smiled, stating that he had worked the overnight shift for quite some time and that the home was kind of spooky when it was all closed up and dark. We didn't press him any further and bade him goodbye, our initial suspicions somewhat confirmed.

Is Beauvoir haunted? My official statement as a paranormal investigator is that it is possible and that only an extensive overnight investigation would confirm or disprove it. My personal opinion is that I am pretty darned sure it is.

THE OLD BILOXI CEMETERY

Sitting right off Beach Boulevard just to the east of the Elks Lodge is the Old Biloxi Cemetery. Officially listed as being at 1166 Irish Hill Drive, the cemetery runs from Highway 90/Beach Boulevard across Irish Hill Drive, crosses the railroad tracks and continues on for a bit. It backs up to the Keesler AFB fence on the west and a neighborhood to the north; this section of the cemetery is somewhat newer than the beachfront area. An extremely old cemetery, no one knows just exactly when the first burial took place. The fact that it is some of the highest ground around and would have been a prime burial location for early settlers would lead one to believe that it was used as a graveyard nearly from the start. That there were already graves on it when the Fayard family deeded it to the city in 1844 as a burying ground was a known fact. The oldest surviving headstone in the Old Biloxi Cemetery belongs to Michel Batet, who was born in France and who died in May 1811 at age thirty-four; his headstone is written in French and today is partially embedded in a dead tree stump.

Crypts in the Old Biloxi Cemetery from the 1800s. It is the final resting place of 12,192 souls, with the earliest known burial being dated in May 1811. *Photo by the author.*

It would also be a likely spot for the poor wretches of the John Law Concessions to be buried. Hundreds of land speculators from several European countries were dropped here thinking that they were coming to the Promised Land. Instead, when they arrived they found very little food

A view of the Old Biloxi Cemetery at night. When the sun goes down, the place takes on an entirely different feel, one of being watched and of someone standing close to you the entire time. *Photo by the author.*

and nearly no development of any kind. The ill-equipped settlers died by the hundreds, maybe even thousands, from 1719 to 1721. It has been speculated that the high bluffs where the Old Biloxi Cemetery sits today would have been the perfect burial place for the poor wretches who didn't survive, although it really is nothing more than educated speculation at best.

Regardless of who the unfortunate individual was who had the misfortune to be the first to take up residence in the graveyard or even when that might have been, one thing is for certain: the cemetery is home to 12,192 known residents, some of whom have been hanging out there for around two hundred years.

During the daylight hours, it's a nice quiet cemetery, well cared for and with few visitors; those who do come are the curious, checking for unusual headstones or just taking a quiet walk away from the constant noise along the beach. At night, however, it takes on a completely different feel. The electricity in the air is nearly palpable. Officially, the cemetery closes at 7:00 p.m. each night, but it isn't unusual to find a car or even the occasional person cutting through the cemetery from Irish Hill to Beach Boulevard in the later hours of the night. While the police keep a pretty good eye on what's going on, if you're not bothering anything, they usually won't bother you. Start messing around and doing something that you shouldn't and the police will haul you off to jail pretty darned quick though—unless, of course, the residents take matters into their own lifeless hands.

While I was living in Biloxi in the 1980s, I was told a story by a young woman who supposedly got the information firsthand from her brother, a trouble-seeking young man who had problems staying out of jail. The group that he hung out with was all cut from the same cloth: wannabe hoods bent on showing everyone how tough they were, legends in their own minds, it would seem. They had been in and out of jail for theft and other small crimes, and it was only a matter of time before they escalated their crimes to include something worse. Hanging out on the beach each evening across from the cemetery, they noticed a young woman who would emerge from the cemetery, hang a right and start down Beach Boulevard heading west. They noticed this several nights in a row and got the idea in their collective heads that she would be an easy mark, so they decided that they would hide out in the cemetery and wait for her the next night. They hid out beside some of the older crypts in the old part of the cemetery, figuring that the noise from Beach Boulevard would mask any noise that she might make when they sprang their attack. Like clockwork, the young lady came hurrying through the cemetery, and when she came abreast of their hiding spots, they sprang out and seized her, shoving her up against a crypt. The "tough guys" then slapped her a few times just to "get her attention," knocking her to the ground beside the crypt. While one was rummaging through her purse, the other two noticed that she was an extremely good-looking girl, and things started to escalate from just a robbery to a rape. The young woman cried out for help but was struck across the face a few more times, stunning her, while the rapists tore at her clothes.

Suddenly, one of the thugs let out a horrified scream, and when the other two turned around, they saw the figure of a man standing behind him, his arm thrust completely through the terrified guy, who by this time was starting to sink slowly to the ground, having fainted at the sight of the arm sticking out of his chest. The other two jumped to their feet to face the assailant, all thoughts of toughness having flown right out the window at the sight of their friend passed out on the ground in an ever-widening puddle of urine. They tried talking their way out of it, promising to leave, but the man never said a word, just sprang at them with unbelievable speed, darting from one to the other. A slap here, a punch there—the man beat them both like the cur dogs they were, moving so fast that they could barely keep up with where he was at, let alone mount some kind of defense. When finally he ceased his assault, they were both on the ground, barely conscious and afraid to even try to move for fear he would set upon them again. He bent over my friend's brother, grabbed him by the shirt front and raised him up to where they were almost nose to nose. He never said a word, just stared at him for a moment or two and then let him go. The would-be tough guy watched from the ground as the man whispered something to the poor young girl on the ground and then extended his hand to help her to her feet. She gathered herself together, picked up her things and, in what I thought was a good touch to the story, kicked my friend's brother squarely between the legs and hurriedly walked away. That left only the three would-be rapists—two beaten severally and one passed out with wet pants—and the young woman's savior. My friend's brother later told his sister that he thought he was going to die right then and there from the look on the man's face, but the man never moved an inch toward them. Instead, he just started a long, low rush of what must have been curses in French directed at the three, spat in their direction and slowly faded away right before their eyes. The so-called tough guys hurriedly gathered up their still passed-out friend and fled the cemetery, only to be picked up later for assault, attempted robbery and attempted rape.

My friend's brother described the ghost to his sister as being a rather nondescript sort of fellow in old-fashioned clothes, with long hair tied back.

Dave Harkins of TOPS (The Ozarks Paranormal Society) taking photos in the Old Biloxi Cemetery at night. He later had scratch marks appear on his arm from out of nowhere. *Photo by the author.*

He was also incredibly fast. He struck hard and without mercy, yet when it was over, he showed kindness and courtesy to the young lady. He was a true gentleman; the mortal world could use a few more just like him. It would seem that the spirit who came to the young woman's assistance could not and would not tolerate a woman being abused in his presence and meted out swift justice in return. Sadly, my friend's brother didn't learn from his mistakes, and following his release from jail, he attempted a robbery again, only to be shot and killed by his would-be victim.

Numerous other spirits have been sighted at the Old Biloxi Cemetery, including what those who have seen him call the "Preacher." Dressed in a black suit and carrying a Bible, he is described as an older fellow with thin hair and sharp, almost hatchet-like features. He will suddenly appear as if from nowhere, asking the startled person if he "knows the Lord," and then proceed to start preaching up a hellfire and brimstone sermon for a few moments before disappearing just as quickly as he appeared, leaving the person confused, unnerved and ready to beat a hasty retreat from the cemetery. He always seems to appear, as the story goes, in the evenings and to people who are alone. He never seems to bother anyone physically; he just seems to profess a sincere concern for their souls, in a creepy sort of way.

When Dave Harkins and I visited the Old Biloxi Cemetery at night, it was just before a huge thunderstorm blew in from off the Gulf. The electricity in the air, while always seeming to be there, had multiplied extensively to where the hair seemed to constantly stand up on our arms. We took some photos in the old section to see if we might capture anything; unfortunately, all we got was orbs, in which neither of us places much faith, as any number of environmental factors can explain them away. Dave was taking a photo and did hear what sounded like metal clinking or change rattling right next to him although no one was there. When I walked over to the spot, I immediately got a creeped-out feeling, as if something was standing right next to me and it wasn't very nice. We snapped a few more photos and then piled into the van to try to beat the storm back to the casino when Dave started to feel a burning on his arm and red marks appeared on his forearm. As we were driving out of the cemetery, I happened to glance over to the left, and in the lightning flash I saw the figure of a man standing beside one of the crypts. I stopped the van and backed up to get another look, but no one was there. Dave caught just a quick glimpse of it too, and unable to see anyone around the area, we went ahead and left.

Are there spirits in the Old Biloxi Cemetery? Well, if the stories are to be believed, then yes there are. My own personal opinion is that there are a bunch of spirits still in the old cemetery—some nice, some not so nice—so if you are planning on visiting the cemetery after dark, take care and be prepared to see something that you just might not want to see.

TULLIS-TOLEDANO HOME

This home was completely destroyed by Hurricane Katrina when she ripped a casino barge loose from its moorings and ran it through the home, depositing it right on the foundation. Nothing is left now, and no plans to rebuild have been mentioned, but one would have to wonder what happened to the ghost. Was he permanently displaced by the storm and carried away to his final rest, or does he still lurk the grounds where the home once stood, lost and unsure of what to do now that the manor no longer exists?

The manor was built in 1856 by Christoval Toledano as a gift for his bride, Ms. Matilde Pradat. It was beautifully built in the Greek Revival style and served the couple well, staying in the family until it was bought by Garner H. Tullis, then president of the New Orleans Cotton Exchange, as

The Tullis-Toledano House was once a favorite place for couples to get married; unfortunately, during Katrina, a casino barge was ripped loose from its moorings and ended up on top of the house, completely destroying it. *Courtesy of the Library of Congress, call #HABS MISS,24-BILX,4-3.*

a summer home in 1939. It remained in their family for some time and was restored after Hurricane Camille did significant damage to it in 1969. It was purchased by the City of Biloxi in 1975 and was used as a museum and local tourist attraction. It was also a favorite place for weddings.

It was also the site of a deadly duel, according to local legend, and the story has been told several different ways; the following is the one I like the best. In or around 1876, the Toledano family was playing host to a family friend, a distinguished young man from New Orleans. A wealthy and handsome young man, he was said to be one of those truly nice people whose wealth and looks seem not to play a huge part in their egos. He believed himself to be the equal of any man and no better than anyone. While staying at the manor, he made the acquaintance of a local young lady who was renowned not only for her great beauty but also for being extremely spoiled and self-centered. She immediately set her cap for the unfortunate young fellow and set about trying to become the sole object of his affection. The young man was no one's fool and saw completely through her less-than-pure intentions. He politely ignored her for the most part and tried valiantly to dodge her advances, but it soon became apparent that he was going to have to firmly make it understood that he was simply not interested in her.

Well, once told, the young woman flew into a fit of rage, unable to comprehend that he wasn't completely enamored with her. She sought out one of her many other suitors, a young man known to have a temper and a nearly unmatched skill with weapons. This young man was unable to see that he was being played and immediately rushed over to the manor to confront the dastardly cretin who had the audacity to rebuff the woman he loved. I would imagine that it never actually occurred to him that he was her second choice, seeing it only as an opportunity to ingratiate himself with the spoiled young girl. The wealthy young man tried to explain the situation to the hot-tempered guy but just couldn't seem to make him understand what was actually going on behind the scenes. An insult was hurled, and one followed back on its heels, and before anyone even realized it, the hot-tempered young man had challenged the Toledanos' visitor to a duel to defend not only his honor but also that of the lady whose advances had been scorned. Everyone present—except the young lady, of course—tried to persuade the hot-tempered young man to let it pass and not follow through with the duel, but he knew that his skill with weapons was great, and he had little doubt that he would prevail and then the young lady would turn her attentions to him.

They agreed to meet within the hour at the back of the house to settle the matter once and for all. Both showed up at the appointed time and prepared to face off, with the chosen weapon being swords—not pistols, as one other version of the story claims. The young man from New Orleans pleaded with the other to reconsider. The hothead, in his arrogance, saw the other's pleas as a sign of weakness and fear and promised to dispatch him quickly with a single thrust to the heart. The battle began, and much to the surprise of the arrogant local guy, the young man from New Orleans was no slouch with a blade, drawing blood from the local boy almost immediately. This should have been the end of the contest, but as the young man from New Orleans turned away, the girl screamed at her admirer to kill him. The hotheaded young man, unable to believe that he had been bested by the other man and following the urgings of the wicked girl behind him, sprang at the man from New Orleans, attempting to run him through as promised. Well, it just wasn't his day at all, it would seem, and the young man from New Orleans, in defense of his life, dispatched the other man with a swift thrust to his chest. As he lay there dying, the rash young man could scarcely believe his eyes as the girl rushed to the side of the victor, professing her love for him and asking forgiveness. As he drew his last breath, he cursed himself for a fool and asked forgiveness from the victor, who, saddened that he had to kill the young man over nothing, quickly granted it to him.

From that point forward, the ghost of the slain duelist would appear from time to time, pacing back and forth in the yard behind the home. People who have witnessed him say that he has a large stain of blood on the front of his shirt and appears to be quite sad. Several people have approached him, thinking that he was injured, only to have him fade away before their eyes. He doesn't seem to like contact with people, and I know of only one story in which he actually addressed someone. A wedding party was taking place on the grounds, and everything was in turmoil, with people rushing to get last-minute things taken care of and friends and family trying to calm the jitters in both bride and groom. The groom excused himself, saying that he wanted to be alone for a few moments, and walked around the house to a more private setting. He was having second thoughts about going through with the wedding and was actually on the verge of cutting and running. As he stood there talking out loud to himself, he suddenly became aware of someone standing next to him. Being a little ticked that someone would interrupt him, he turned to see who it was. It turned out to be none other than the duelist, bloodstained shirt and all. He quietly told the young man that he was blessed to have found love, to treasure it above all else and that life was way too short to spend wondering if you were making the right decision. He stated that he had chosen wrongly and paid the price but that the groom had chosen wisely and would have a lifetime of happiness. With that said, the duelist turned to leave and vanished before the startled groom's eyes. The groom did indeed take the advice and married the young woman; as to the lifetime of happiness part, one can only hope the spirit was correct.

THE BILOXI LIGHTHOUSE

Built in 1848 for the purpose of guiding fishermen and mariners home from the sea, the Biloxi Lighthouse has withstood the forces of Mother Nature, taking only minimal damage from the abundant hurricanes and tropical storms that plague the area. It has witnessed occupation by Union troops, building of roadways and a pristine white sand beach, countless families and young people enjoying the Gulf—and at least one reported suicide.

The Biloxi Lighthouse, 2012. It is thought to be the most photographed object in the South. *Photo by the author.*

The story goes that in the late 1860s to early 1870s, a man had invested heavily in a local business. Unfortunately, the owner of the business wasn't as much a businessman as a con man, and the poor fellow ended up losing everything that he had. Left with nothing and facing what he believed to be public humiliation, it was more than the poor guy could take, so he climbed up the lighthouse stairs to the top, tied a rope around the railing and promptly hanged himself. People say that on moonlit nights you can see the shadow of someone walking around the upper floor of the lighthouse and around the outside railing. More than one accounting has been told of a tourist taking a photo of the lighthouse at night only to review it later and find the form of a man looking out the windows of the locked lighthouse. You would have to feel sorry for the fellow, checking out of life like that only to end up hanging around a lighthouse for eternity.

THE OLD BRICK HOUSE

Built around 1850 by John Henley, a former sheriff and mayor of Biloxi, on land that was originally granted to Jean Baptiste Carquotte in 1784 by the Spanish government, this historic home sits at 622 Bayview Drive in Biloxi and overlooks the Back Bay. This is one of the oldest—if not *the* oldest—homes remaining in Biloxi and was placed on the National Register of Historic Places in 1973. The home was salvaged by the Biloxi Garden Clubs around 1950, after it had suffered a period of neglect and was in pretty bad shape. It was later acquired by the City of Biloxi to serve as a museum and a place for public gatherings and receptions. Severely damaged when Hurricane Katrina hit, it was under seven feet of water during the storm surge. The sturdy construction of Mr. Henley, who used tough heart pine lumber for the flooring and three layers of brick in the walls, allowed it to survive the storm. Since then, it has been restored to be historically accurate—so accurate that perhaps one of the old occupants still thinks it's his.

The figure of a man in the formal attire of a gentleman from the late 1800s has been seen on more than one occasion standing on the front porch looking out over the Back Bay of Biloxi. Smoking a pipe while standing there, this figure will suddenly knock out his pipe, turn and walk through the front door to the interior of the home. And when I say walk *through* the front door, that's exactly what I mean. He walks right through the closed front

The Old Brick House on the Back Bay of Biloxi was built around 1850 by John Henley, a former sheriff and mayor of Biloxi. *Photo by the author.*

door as if it isn't even there. Who he is no one seems to know, and he is an infrequent visitor, showing up to smoke his pipe and then walk through the door at almost any time, with no rhyme or reason to his sudden appearance. He never interacts with anyone but just seems to be enjoying his pipe and the view. He has also been seen at times standing in the yard only to disappear in the blink of an eye when seen.

BILOXI NATIONAL CEMETERY

Established on the grounds of the VA Medical Center in 1934, the Biloxi National Cemetery was originally intended as a burial place for those who passed away at the medical facility. From 1934 to 1973, that was its sole purpose, and when the National Cemetery Act was passed in 1973, it was opened to any honorably discharged veteran or active duty personnel and their dependents. It has increased in size twice and now contains fifty-four acres at the VA for the express purpose of veterans' burials. It contains the remains of one Medal of Honor winner, Colonel Ira C. Welborn of the

The Biloxi National Cemetery, final resting place of our nation's veterans and their families since 1934. *Photo by the author.*

Spanish-American War. It also contains the graves of six unknown soldiers; their remains are from the Mexican-American War, and their caskets started washing out of the beach at Greenwood Island near Pascagoula, Mississippi, the site of Camp Jefferson Davis. They were reinterred at the Biloxi National Cemetery with full military honors.

Many times over the years, people have reported apparitions both at the cemetery and at the medical facility. Stories of soldiers in dress uniforms suddenly appearing in the cemetery only to disappear just as quickly were pretty commonplace during World War II, Korea and most especially after Vietnam, when it seemed that a rash of sightings of young men in uniform broke out. One story tells of a family visiting the grave of a loved one who became suddenly aware that someone was standing a little to the side of them. Supposedly the young man, in dress greens with spit-shined low quarters, apologized for bothering them and then asked for a light. As the man lit his cigarette, the family noticed the name tag on his uniform said Jones and asked if he was there visiting a comrade. The young soldier smiled and said, "Not really," thanked them for the light and then walked away, only to disappear right before their eyes.

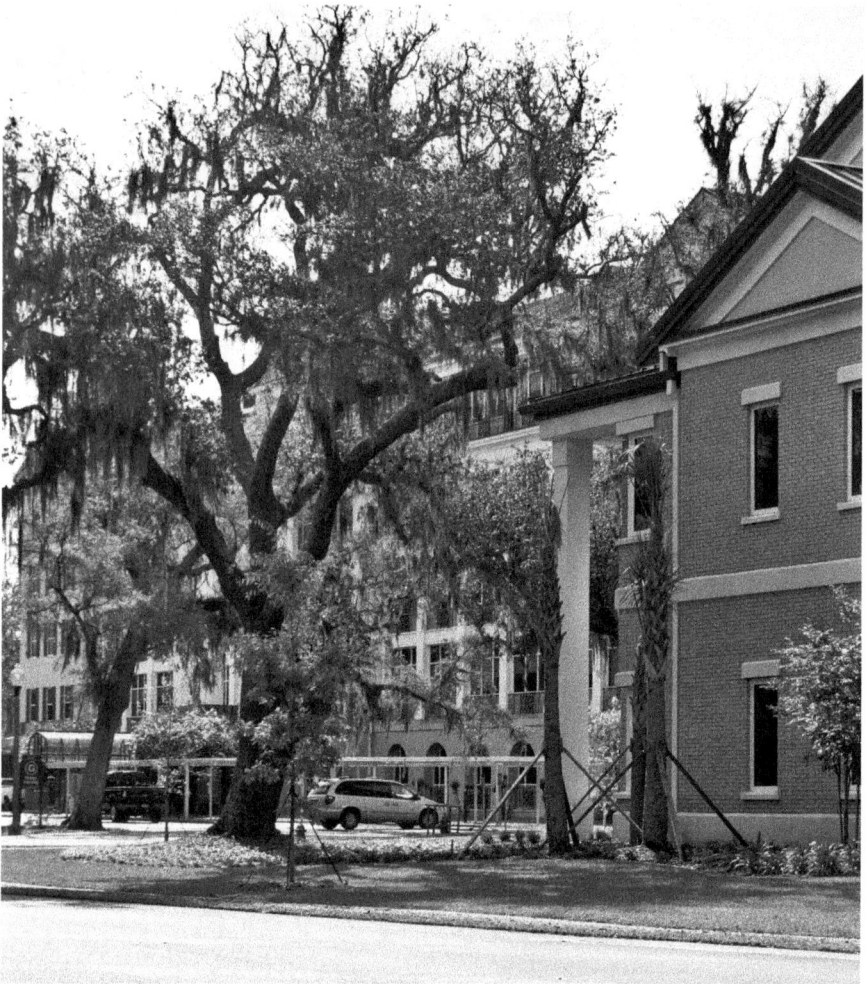

The Veterans' Hospital in Biloxi, supposedly home to a prankster spirit by the name of "Mr. Frank." *Photo by the author.*

Strange things have happened in the medical facility as well over the years. One story was told for quite some time about "Mr. Frank," a jovial spirit that liked to move things around on the nurses and play other pranks. Supposedly he was a patient there in the 1960s who was struck with a terminal disease that was slowly driving him down. He was said to always have a smile or laugh, even at the end. While he was still mobile, he would walk the halls in his gown, dragging an IV pole along with him, the back of his gown wide open and exposing his buttocks for all to see. He would stop at the nurses' station to play a joke or two on them before strolling on down the hallway. After he passed away, the nurses kept noticing things being moved or disappearing altogether, only to reappear right where they had been left before, and always when no one was looking. They started saying that Mr. Frank was messing with them, and that got to be the running joke whenever they couldn't find something. Mr. Frank got the last laugh on them though when one of the nurses misplaced the keys to the narcotics cabinet. Frantically searching for them, she muttered softly that she wished Mr. Frank would "stop all the BS and just give her the darned keys back." No sooner had she said that than the keys suddenly appeared in midair in front of her and dropped to the floor with a bang. The startled woman bent down to pick up the keys and felt someone pat her on the backside. Straightening up and spinning around to give some doctor or resident a piece of her mind, she came face to face with the grinning Mr. Frank, who simply winked at her and disappeared. The woman, understandably shaken, ran from the nurses' station in hysterics. She took quite a while to calm down and even longer before she would work that station alone.

MARY MAHONEY'S OLD FRENCH HOUSE RESTAURANT

The exact date that the Old French House was built is unknown, but some believe that it was built sometime around the early to mid-1700s. The building—now known as Mary Mahoney's Old French House Restaurant—sits at 110 Rue Magnolia in Biloxi, a short walk up from the beach. Bob and Mary Mahoney, along with her brother-in-law Andrew Cvitanovich, bought, remodeled and opened the structure as a restaurant in 1964, and it still remains in the family today, serving fresh coastal cuisine as it has for over forty-eight years. People absolutely love to come to Mary's, and it has been a tradition on the coast for generations. Some people like it so well that they never seem to leave.

One story about Mary's is of the ghost in the mirror. For years now, the story has persisted that whenever a woman would enter the ladies' room at Mary Mahoney's, the reflection that she would see looking back at her from the mirror might not be her own. No one knows who the reflection is, and as far as I know, she has never attempted to make contact with anyone. The lady patron would simply look down, and when she looked back up, there would be a reflection of the young woman looking back out at her—never moving, never speaking, simply looking out the mirror at the patron. Naturally, this

Mary Mahoney's Old French House Restaurant, one of the oldest buildings in Biloxi, is said to be home to a spirit who likes to look at you from the bathroom mirrors. *Photo by the author.*

has caused more than one lady to beat a hasty retreat from the restaurant, shaken up and demanding to know if there is a two-way mirror in the ladies' room. There was a story told that a man, looking in the mirror in the men's room, spotted the young woman looking back out at him. Startled at first, he tried to elicit a response or some movement from the girl, but after a few moments of trying, he gave up and left, chalking it up to an optical illusion based on poor lighting and old mirrors. I know after hearing that she put in an appearance in the men's room, whenever I happen to go in there I take extra care, just in case anyone's watching.

CHAPTER 7
OCEAN SPRINGS

O cean Springs was the site of the first French settlement on the Mississippi Gulf Coast, then called Fort Maurepas. Established by D'Iberville in 1699, it was the first French toehold on the coast and was key in maintaining control of the vast land claims made by France. Easily gotten to by boat from the deep-water anchorage at Ship Island and sitting on relatively high ground, it was both accessible and defendable.

Even though the settlement was moved to near Mobile and then back to Ocean Springs before finally being moved across the bay to Biloxi and then on to New Orleans, there was pretty much a French presence and settlement at Ocean Springs since D'Iberville first landed. Several people established homes close to the old fort, including Madam Bodron, Littlepage Robertson, Woodsen Wren and a man named Louis Auguste LaFontaine, who purchased the land where the center of Ocean Springs is today. Once the area came under control of the United States, more and more Americans moved into the area and established homes, farms and businesses. Residents of the area lived by harvesting seafood and lumber and farming, as well as the export of charcoal. Many schooner loads of charcoal and lumber sailed from Ocean Springs to New Orleans, and the little community on the east shore of the bay continued to thrive and grow.

Mineral springs were discovered, and several hotels sprang up as the springs were exploited as a cure-all. Many people came and stayed in the hotels while seeking hydrotherapy for all sorts of physical discomforts. One such hotel, the Ocean Springs Hotel, was where the city took its name from in 1854, having briefly been known as Lynchburg Springs when the first post office was opened in 1853. A small tourist trade centered on the mineral springs and the cool ocean breezes developed and stayed steady right up until the Civil War. The war affected Ocean Springs as it did the rest of the coast, with food being in short supply. What there was to be had was way overpriced. People fished and hunted for food, and chickens and eggs were raised and harvested, so all in all, compared to the rest of the South, the residents of Ocean Springs got along pretty well.

After the Civil War, life picked back up, and slowly the tourist trade resumed, with people once again coming to the spas. With the establishment of the railroad, people could travel more easily to Ocean Springs. Eventually, some nice estates were developed along the east beach by wealthy families from New Orleans and businessmen from the North, as the area was recognized as a beautiful place to settle. The slow pace of life with the cool Gulf breezes made the area very attractive.

Having always had a good fishing industry, the establishment of packing plants in Biloxi and Gulfport helped to grow the industry into a very solid business. Numerous fishing boats and fleets were based out of Ocean Springs, and even today you can easily purchase fresh fish, shrimp and oysters from local fisherman, fresh off the boat. Excess seafood was sold to the packing plants in the area, and demand was always good for fresh Gulf seafood, providing a good steady income for local fishermen.

Ocean Springs survived both world wars much the same as the rest of the coast, and many men and women enlisted to fight for freedom or to support the troops. When the fighting had stopped and the people came home, Ocean Springs was a haven to more than one veteran looking to experience a slower, easier lifestyle and a way to forget the horrors of war and ease back into civilian life. The population increased slowly over those years, and businesses were started and grown. The laid-back feeling of Ocean Springs contributed greatly to the slow but steady growth. Tourism continued, not so much due to the mineral springs any longer but in part because Americans wanted to play. Cars were more easily accessible, roads had improved and the lure of the sea pulled many vacationers to the Gulf Coast. People came to visit and ended up staying, enamored with the lifestyle and climate.

Ocean Springs was severely damaged by both Hurricanes Camille and Katrina, like the rest of the Gulf Coast, but it has since rebounded, and with the reopening of the bridge on Highway 90 from Biloxi to Ocean Springs, life has returned to normal for the most part. Ocean Springs is now known as an arts community, with several art galleries and shops showcasing local artists' work lining the downtown areas. Once home to artist Walter Inglis Anderson, a nationally known painter and muralist who died in 1965 from lung cancer, the city holds several arts festivals each year, including an Herb Festival, celebrating all different types of naturally grown herbs. All in all, Ocean Springs is a remarkable place to call home and a great place to visit, with easy access to the coast and New Orleans. Many who come to visit end up moving there to stay—even after they have passed on.

ROCK AND ROLL GRAVEYARD

The William Seymour Cemetery, otherwise known as the Rock and Roll Graveyard, sits just north of Ocean Springs near the junction of Fort Bayou Road and Bayou Talla. If you turn off Fort Bayou onto Bayou Talla, you will dead-end right into the cemetery. A very nice, secluded cemetery, it has been the subject of many stories and legends, some of them so bizarre you wonder how they ever started. This cemetery, by the way, is private property

The William Seymour Cemetery, also known as the Rock and Roll Graveyard, is the home of many strange tales, including one of a hanging man. If you count the curves in the road going in you will get fourteen, but on the way out, you will only count thirteen for some reason. *Photo by the author.*

and very well patrolled by the police. Dave Harkins and I went to check it out for ourselves, and as we were leaving, we had a police officer pass us on Bayou Talla on his way in to check on the property. (As with any private property, especially family burial grounds, be respectful and ask for permission before just taking it upon yourselves to trespass.) We had heard all about the bizarre stories and wanted to see for ourselves, but unfortunately, access to the cemetery after dark is forbidden, so we had to do our checking in the daylight hours.

One thing that I can say about the area is that even in the daylight, the road going in and out has an unusual feel to it, like something is not quite right or that you are being watched; I couldn't really put my finger on it. We had heard the stories of the number of curves being different going in than coming out and decided that we would see if that was the case or if it was just another urban legend. From the start of Bayou Talla, we carefully counted the curves going in, making sure that we were in agreement as to what constituted a curve and what was just a slight bend in the roadway. We wanted to be sure we were in absolute agreement so as to be as precise as possible with our count. We slowly drove the uneasy-feeling road back to the cemetery and counted fourteen curves total going in. We took some photos and did a short EVP session at the cemetery, both of us remarking that we really didn't feel uneasy at the place. In fact, it was actually pretty peaceful and quiet. We poked around for about an hour before leaving and starting our count of the curves again. Slowly, we drove back down the road, making sure to count each curve as meticulously as we had driving in, and as we got to the last curve, we both stopped and looked at each other in disbelief. We counted only *thirteen* curves coming out! Where the fourteenth curve went we have absolutely no darned idea, but we were extremely careful in our count. And even odder still is that if you go to Google Earth to get an earth view, you will count only eleven curves total. How this is I have absolutely no idea, but this is one legend about the Rock and Roll Graveyard that I can't disprove.

Stories about the graveyard are many, with one of the most famous being the lady in the rocking chair. The story goes that if you visit the cemetery in the late hours of the night, you will see the old lady in white rocking slowly back and forth in her rocker just inside the gate. She is said to appear only *after* you have entered the cemetery by the gate, effectively putting herself between you and the way out. She is said to rock and rock, back and forth, slowly rocking closer and closer to you, never saying a word. Of course, many who have seen her haven't stayed around to visit with her but have jumped the fence to get away.

The Rock and Roll Graveyard near Ocean Springs, Mississippi. *Photo by the author.*

Another story is that of the hanging man. Supposedly, a local man was distraught over something and decided to cash in his chips and end it all. He drove to the cemetery, went to the big tree just inside the fence, threw a rope over the limb and proceeded to go about the business of hanging himself. According to the story, this happened in August, which is an extremely hot and humid month, and the man wasn't missed for a few days. When someone finally drove back to the cemetery, they reportedly found him swinging gently in the breeze, parts of him missing either from animals or who knows what and in a very rapid state of decomposition. When the coroner arrived to take him down, apparently his body, bloated from the heat, just gave out and ruptured, spilling his innards all over the ground and the coroner. Supposedly to this day, if you go back to the graveyard on a hot August afternoon, you just might see the specter of the hanging man swinging from the tree limb where he hanged himself. Others have reported the smell of rotting flesh whenever they walk close to the tree, only to have it disappear completely as they walk a few feet away.

One of the most bizarre stories, though, is that of the albinos. Local legend has it that a family of albinos lives near the cemetery, keeping watch over it and attacking any unfortunate soul who dares to trespass alone. Reported to be hatchet-swinging red-eyed cannibals who will kill you and then harvest a few parts for a snack, they have been reportedly seen by dozens of people who have dared to drive Bayou Talla Road. Most people chalk this story up to nothing more than urban legend and scoff about it, pointing out that if there was a family of flesh-eating albinos living out in the woods, how come no one but a bunch of scared partiers has seen them? A valid point, I must confess, and one that I tend to favor myself, but true or not, one thing is a definite fact: Bayou Talla Road is one weird piece of roadway.

THE EAST BEACH

Driving from Highway 90, if you take Holcomb Boulevard or Bechtel Boulevard and head south, you will run right into East Beach Drive and the beach and shoreline that border it. A nice beach with views of the casinos and shoreline of Biloxi, it is a quiet place to walk and relax. In the early morning hours, it is common to see people jogging along the beach or simply sitting and watching the day come alive. Ocean Springs is a safe place to hang out, and its beaches are rarely crowded with tourists, who seem to like to stay on the beaches as close to their hotels and casinos as possible, so the people that you find along the beach at Ocean Springs are mostly locals.

One of the stories of the east beach is that of the ghostly runner. Said to be a young woman dressed in running attire and wearing a baseball cap, she is said to suddenly appear out of nowhere, smile and say hi as she passes by, only to disappear a few feet from you. The startled people who have seen her have no idea who she is but remarked that she seemed very pleasant and had a very engaging smile. That she speaks and nods to you as she passes would lead me to believe that she is an intelligent haunting rather than a residual spirit, and I can only surmise that she must have loved running along the east beach so much in life that she just continues on with it in death.

Another story told to me about the east beach is that of the "settler," called that because of his clothing, which resembles what some have called pioneer clothes. He is said to be seen just as the sun is setting, wandering along as if he had not a care in the world nor any place to be. He obviously doesn't care for company at all and, if approached, will simply fade away, his tracks still visible at the water's edge. One person approached him only to have him disappear, leaving the person a bit confused for a moment. When the person turned around to leave, he spotted him again a bit farther down the beach, just walking along as if enjoying the sunset.

CHAPTER 8
GAUTIER

N amed for the family who founded a sawmill business in the area, Gautier (pronounced GO-shay) is a nice little bedroom community that boasts two championship golf courses and is home to historic homes and properties, all surrounded on three sides by wetlands. Though settled by Fernando Upton Gautier in 1867, the town of Gautier was not incorporated until 1986 and is listed as one of the fifty largest cities in Mississippi. All through the late 1800s up until World War II, it remained a small, rural community, but with the establishment of the naval shipyards at Pascagoula, it started to grow as shipbuilders employed at the yard soon recognized the benefits of living in the quiet town.

The city experienced nice steady growth through the years, with a total population, according to the 2000 census, of 11,681, although the annexation of land around Gautier raised the population to somewhere around 18,413 people. With good overall schools, convenience to Pascagoula and other large coastal cities and plenty of recreation opportunities, the projected growth of Gautier is expected to fall somewhere around 22,800 people by 2025. Still, even with the increase in population and development that Gautier has already experienced, it has managed to maintain the charm of small-town living, making it an extremely attractive place to be. So attractive, in fact, that some people have decided to stay around forever.

THE OLD PLACE

The homestead built by Fernando Upton Gautier in 1867 still stands today, known to the local population as the Old Place. He moved into the area from New Orleans after the Civil War came to a close and established a thriving sawmill business. From that business sprang the town of Gautier, so named on the maps of the time due to the family name being marked on the sawmill water tower. With the successful and lucrative business supplying a decent income, Gautier built a spacious home on the banks of the Singing River and, with his wife, Theresa Fayard Gautier, set about raising their family. The home is still owned by their descendants and is used today for both public and private events.

Across Highway 90 from the Old Place sets the Gautier Family Cemetery, ringed now by a rusting chain-link fence and overgrown with vines in spots, although the cemetery itself is very well cared for. Several stories surround both the Old Place and the graveyard, most specifically the supposed hanging tree located just inside the cemetery fence. The story goes that even before the Gautier's settled on the west bank of the Singing River, several families had lived there since almost the beginning of French settlement. They eked

A side view of the Old Place in Gautier, Mississippi. It has been in the same family since it was built in 1867 by Fernando Gautier. The yard is where the spirits of a man and woman are said to stroll arm in arm. *Photo by the author.*

out a living by farming and producing charcoal that was then shipped from Ocean Springs. According to the stories, one family owned several slaves, and the patriarch of the family, who was known to be a cruel and vicious sort of fellow, would get his enjoyment by abusing his slaves. He would take them out to the hanging tree—now located at the Gautier Family Cemetery—tie them to the tree and set about beating them with a whip, although some versions of the story are much more gruesome and perverted. When he finally wore the slaves out from mistreatment and too much work, he would take them again to the tree and hang them as a warning to the other slaves that he was the master, which in his sick and twisted mind put him on the same level with God, and that they were compelled to do his every bidding. When he would tire of seeing them swinging in the breeze from the great tree limb, he would have other slaves bury them close by, which is where the story of the property already being used as a graveyard before the Gautier's took over the land most likely stemmed from. People say that if you go out by the graveyard on an overcast night, when the moon happens to peek through the clouds you can sometimes see the bodies of the slaves hanging from the limbs of the great old tree. The sounds of a whip and the screams and crying of someone in extreme pain have been reported to be heard as well, although those who have reported hearing them have said that they were very faint and sounded as if they were coming from far away. Perhaps they are a residual effect left over from a place that witnessed so much pain and suffering.

Back across the highway at the Old Place, the spirits of a man and woman have been seen both together and separately. When seen together, they are strolling arm in arm around the grounds, mostly in the very early morning or late evening, apparently taking a nice, quiet stroll. They seem to be enjoying each other's company immensely, laughing and chatting as they walk. They are only glimpsed for a few moments before fading away in an almost whitish type of mist. The woman, when seen alone, is usually standing on the back porch gazing out at the Singing River as if in deep thought. Described by those who have seen her as being in her late thirties and dressed in an off-white dress with a high collar, she has been said to be quite a handsome woman; some have described her as being "breathtakingly beautiful" even. Who she is no one knows, but perhaps she is one of the Gautier's who loved the beautiful home so much that she just didn't want to ever leave it. Or maybe she is Theresa Fayard Gautier and the man is Fernando; said to be so much in love when alive, maybe they cling to each other's spirits in death. The man, when seen alone, is merely walking across the back of the property by the riverbank, as if off on some task, as his pace has been described as that of someone who is moving

The supposed "Hanging Tree" at the Gautier Family Cemetery, where a local man was said to beat and torture his worn-out slaves before hanging them. *Photo by the author.*

with a purpose. He has been described as a man of medium height with short, dark hair and a mustache. Dressed well but not overly dignified, and with his shirtsleeves rolled up as if he has been working, he is said to be rather serious looking. Neither of the spirits has ever had any contact with anyone, preferring to be left alone or in each other's company. When seen, they usually disappear after a few moments.

THE SINGING RIVER

The Singing River flows into the Gulf near the town of Gautier, moving along slowly and easily, passing by old homes, new homes and the occasional fish camp before finally merging its waters with that of the sea. The story that is associated with it is both tragic and yet uplifting in a way, establishing love and dedication for one another as a people over life itself. Thinking that they had no hope, they chose to leave this realm on their own terms.

The story is about the Pascagoula Indian tribe, a small and peaceful group who lived along the shores of the Singing River. To the west of them

The Singing River by Gautier runs by the Old Place. Legends hold that the Pascagoula committed mass suicide by drowning rather than face death and slavery at the hands of the Biloxi. *Photo by the author.*

lived the Biloxi tribe, a more warlike nation who considered themselves to be above the other tribes of the area. As the legend goes, a princess of the Biloxi named Anola fell in love with a handsome member of the Pascagoula named Altama, said to be chief of the tribe in some versions of the story. Already promised to another member of the Biloxi, Anola chose instead to abandon her people for love and fled to live among the Pascagoula with Altama. As you can imagine, that did not sit well with the Biloxi, who saw it as a great insult to their people and immediately set out to wage war on the offending Pascagoula. Faced with the choices of giving up the young couple (which would have resulted in Altama's death) or going to war with the Biloxi (which meant almost certain death or enslavement), they chose to back the young lovers. Knowing that they could not defeat the Biloxi and well aware of the consequences of losing the fight, they were determined as a people to decide their own fate. As a group, they joined hands and started walking out into the Singing River, singing their death song as they walked, the entire group united as one. They chose to support the young lovers by choosing a death of their own making by drowning in the river over death or enslavement by the Biloxi.

It is said that if you go down to the river in the evening when all is quiet, you will hear their soft death song coming from the water. A great number of people, including myself, have heard the singing coming from the river; it sounds a little like a buzzing sort of sound, although very melodious. Numerous explanations have been devised over the years to account for the singing, but none of them has ever been proven. I would like to think that perhaps it is the Pascagoula, still united as a people even in death, with the young lovers Anola and Altama leading the chorus, together for all time.

CHAPTER 9

PASCAGOULA

S ituated across the Singing River from Gautier and on the mouth of the bay, Pascagoula is today a major player in the shipbuilding markets. The county seat of Jackson County, it had a population of 26,200 people when the 2000 census was conducted. Before it became a shipbuilding town at the onset of World War II, it was a sleepy little fishing town with barely 5,000 residents total.

Settled by the French, like the rest of the Mississippi Gulf Coast, it was known to have families living on the east side of the river and bay as early as 1718, with the construction of the Old Spanish Fort or, as it is also known, the LaPointe-Krebs House, being finished around the early 1720s. Settlers moved in slowly by all accounts, with only a handful of families living in the area by 1728, but the easy access to the Gulf and the wide rivers attracted more and more settlers, establishing farms and fishing businesses along the bay and farther to the north. The village grew slowly, and by the early 1800s, when the territory became the state of Mississippi, Pascagoula was part of Jackson County. It saw the first schools established around 1818. The first recorded hanging was in 1837 when a man set fire to the courthouse in an attempt to destroy evidence against him in a pig-stealing case. Apparently, pig stealing and arson were taken pretty seriously back then.

Camp Jefferson Davis was established in 1848, after the Mexican-American War came to a close, on Greenwood Island, which was near the village of East Pascagoula. It consisted of a parade ground, officers' quarters, a hospital and storehouses for food and equipment. Death from disease and wounds suffered in the war were not unheard of, and burials were held on the grounds. In 1989, two caskets were found washing out of the ground; the remains were later identified as being from the Camp Jefferson Davis period, although who exactly the men were was never determined. They were later buried with full military honors at the Biloxi National Cemetery along with four other soldiers' bodies that were discovered in the same area of where Camp Jefferson Davis once stood.

When the Civil War broke out, the area around Pascagoula saw a bit more action than the rest of the Mississippi Gulf Coast, with a small naval skirmish out in the sound. In 1863, a troop of black Union soldiers, numbering about 160 men, landed at Pascagoula and drove back a small company of Confederate defenders. They hoisted the Federal flag over the East Pascagoula Hotel for a short time before being driven back to Ship Island, from whence they had come, by a Confederate force from the Mobile area. Other than that and the odd skirmish here and there, the only other real big landing was of Federal troops under Grainger at Pascagoula with the intent to take Mobile. That was largely a flop, and it wasn't very long before they withdrew. After that, it was pretty quiet in Pascagoula throughout the rest of the war.

In about 1870, the railroad came to Pascagoula, making it easier for materials to be brought to the port for export and for passenger service to Mobile and New Orleans. That resulted in a brief increase in residents, some of whom were vacationers, but Pascagoula never saw the influx of tourists like Bay St. Louis or Waveland did. Instead, it grew along the lines of Gulfport, with trade, export and manufacturing taking the lead in growth.

In 1874, a terrible yellow fever epidemic struck Pascagoula, resulting in the deaths of numerous citizens. It even necessitated the quarantining of the port facilities. In 1893, a major hurricane struck, destroying much of the town and killing numerous people, and another one struck in 1906, devastating much of the timber industry and destroying numerous homes and businesses. Again tragedy struck Pascagoula in 1921, when a major fire started in the downtown area and ended up destroying twenty-five businesses and twenty-five homes, although it is not recorded that anyone lost their lives in the destructive blaze.

Despite all the death and rebuilding, Pascagoula struggled on, growing steadily over the years, and in 1938, the Ingalls Shipyard was built. By 1940, it had produced the world's first all-welded ship, which was dedicated and launched on June 8. That was the start of a long line of ships built and repaired at the facility during World War II, and in later years, the facility was modernized and updated to produce some of the finest ships sailing the seas today. The shipyards employ hundreds of workers and are one of the main sources of employment on the coast for welders and electricians. Overall, the economy is doing fairly well in Pascagoula. New jobs are being formed and housing sales are holding their own, so prospects continue to look bright for this city, with continued slow steady growth being projected. With all the history and tragedy the area has faced, the future looks pretty bright for paranormal investigators in Pascagoula too. Many stories of ghosts being seen and haunted buildings and cemeteries abound in the area, and new paranormal groups are established with regular frequency. Maybe one of them will actually catch some hard evidence of the stories that people like to tell about the ghosts of Pascagoula.

THE LONGFELLOW HOUSE

The Longfellow House, also known as Bellevue, was built in 1850 for Daniel Smith Graham, a slave trader and New Orleans businessman. One of the oldest homes along the water in Pascagoula, it has served many purposes over the years. Home to the Pollock/Moore family for a great number of years, it was also used as a girls' school, a resort and private club for Ingalls Shipbuilding Company and even a small resort hotel in the 1940s named the Longfellow House. According to local legend, Henry Wadsworth Longfellow stayed at the hotel when he wrote his work titled *The Building of the Ship*; however, it does seem to be just local legend and nothing more than a marketing attempt to draw guests in the door.

Over the years, the owners of the home made many upgrades and alterations to the property, including aluminum siding for the exterior and modernizing the interior. Left to a period of neglect, it was rescued from demolition by Richard and Diane Scruggs in 1993, and under the direction of the Koch and Wilson Architects firm, Robert Cangelosi was able to both stabilize the home and remove all of the non-historic alterations. The home, now restored to its former glory, was donated by the Scruggs family to the University of Mississippi Foundation and was once again pressed into service as an entertainment facility for public use. Unfortunately, Hurricane Katrina caused considerable damage to the home when it blasted into Pascagoula, and the home was left to sit, waiting for repairs. In 2006, the property was sold to Drs. Randy and

The Longfellow House, 1936. This home received its name from the legend that famous author Henry Wadsworth Longfellow once stayed there while penning *The Building of the Ship*. *Courtesy of the Library of Congress, call #HABS MISS,30-PASCA,5-1.*

Tracy Roth, who restored it and now use it as a private residence, bringing the home full circle back to its original purpose.

Stories associated with the home over the years focused mainly on the original owners. It's said that Ms. Graham was a bit of a cruel mistress where her slaves were concerned and a hard taskmaster. When Mr. Graham would be off on a business trip, she would take that opportunity to indulge her taste for cruelty and take whichever poor unfortunate slave had vexed her up to the attic for a good beating, among other things. She was said to always maintain a kindly appearance to the outside public, which might be where the attic part of the story came into play; it would be easy to hide her penchant for the whip from the public by doling out her punishments in the privacy of the attic. Bloodstains were said to be soaked into the attic floor, permanent reminders of the suffering inflicted there. Ghosts of the tortured and murdered slaves were said to haunt the home, slamming doors, opening cupboards and creating mischief for residents and guests alike. Specters of slaves were seen on the upstairs landing, only to fade away quickly. They were also seen on the grounds, walking and running across the yard, there one second, gone the next, leaving the witnesses to wonder if they had even actually seen them.

THE OLD SPANISH FORT AND CEMETERY

The Old Spanish Fort, otherwise known as the LaPointe-Krebs House, is said to be the oldest standing structure in the state of Mississippi and was erected around 1721. French Canadian Joseph Simon de La Pointe constructed the building first as a carpenter's shop, in which he likely lived while building the main home and the rest of the complex, and as a protection of sorts from the nearby Spanish, hence the "Old Spanish Fort" designation. The Krebs connection comes from one Hugo Ernestus Krebs, who emigrated from Germany to the Pascagoula area and married Marie Josepha Simon, La Pointe's daughter. They raised several sons in the home and were later buried in the cemetery adjacent to the fort.

The home was built of unusual construction, using a material called tabby, which is a concrete type of material made from oyster shells. The thick walls have endured countless hurricanes and tropical storms in surprisingly good shape. The building thought to have been the carpenter's shop is the only surviving building of the complex and has been used as a museum since its restoration.

The Old Spanish Fort Cemetery holds the remains of some of the earliest settlers of the region. This image was taken in 1940. *Courtesy of the Library of Congress, call #HABS MISS,30-PASCA,3-24.*

The Old Spanish Fort, otherwise known as the La Pointe/Krebs House, is thought to be the oldest standing structure on the Gulf Coast. This image was taken in 1940 before restoration was started. *Courtesy of the Library of Congress, call #HABS MISS,30-PASCA,3-5.*

Some of the stories associated with it and the cemetery are most closely associated with the early French settlement. The apparition of a man dressed in clothing said to resemble that of the 1700s has been seen standing on the front porch of the building and was thought at first to be a museum reenactor. Upon inquiry as to where the reenactor had gone to, the people who had seen him were informed that there were no reenactors on the property. He has been seen walking the grounds and at the old cemetery as well, only to disappear a few moments after being seen. Mysterious lights have been seen in the vicinity of the cemetery at night and in the early morning hours, some flitting around, others moving very slowly, as if at a walking pace. Whenever anyone would investigate, they would simply disappear, only to reappear later on after the investigator had walked away.

THE SHIPYARDS

In 1938, the Ingalls Shipyard was built and put into service, completing and launching its first vessel in 1940. It has been in continuous operation since it opened and is the largest employer in Pascagoula, currently employing about ten thousand skilled workers. At its largest during the 1970s, it employed just over twenty-five thousand people, and as you can imagine, with that many people and machines running in one 611-acre complex, accidents were bound to happen; some of them were reported to be deadly. In 1961, Litton Industries acquired Ingalls and expanded the complex, and in 2001, Northrop Grumman Corporation bought out Litton. When Katrina hit in 2005, the facility suffered extensive damage to its buildings, cranes and equipment, and for a brief time, work on the ships was suspended while the facilities were rebuilt. In 2011, Northrop Grumman turned its shipbuilding enterprise into a new company called Huntington Ingalls Industries and continues to operate out of the facilities in Pascagoula.

One of the stories that I like best about ghosts is the one I mentioned in passing at the start of this book: the lunchroom ghost. Having been sighted several times over the last forty years, this particular specter likes to frequent the break room at the shipyards during lunchtime. He seems to wait until the room is crowded before making his appearance, perhaps for maximum

The Pascagoula Shipyards are secure facilities owned by Huntington Ingalls Industries, which repairs and builds ships for the navy and commercial use. *Photo by the author.*

effect. He suddenly appears in the lunch room walking along and takes an empty seat at a table, placing his 1950s-era lunch box on the table before him. He is said to look around and smile at several of the workers, making eye contact with each before opening up his lunch box, looking inside and then fading away with a grimace on his face, perhaps tired of seeing the same old lunch for the past forty years or so. No one knows who he is or why he seems to only frequent the break room on an irregular schedule, but those who have seen him say that he is dressed like a welder, complete with burn marks from slag on his work pants.

One of the oddest stories told to me about the shipyard is that of the little boy bouncing a basketball. Just what a boy would be doing bouncing a basketball around a secure shipbuilding facility is beyond me, but several people have witnessed him, dressed in jeans and a T-shirt, bouncing a basketball as he walks. The sound of the ball was clearly heard by those who saw him, and he apparently walked behind an upright support beam only to disappear on the other side of it, even though the bouncing of the ball was heard to continue on.

Lots of stories about the shipyards are told, some believable and some just outright yarns. Stories of ghosts and phantom workers suddenly appearing or handing a tool to someone are not unheard of. Shadows

A ship at the Pascagoula Shipyards awaiting repair. *Photo by the author.*

walking the property and alarms going off in secure areas when no one is around all lend an air of creepiness to the facility, especially at night. Who the ghostly visitors are is a mystery—perhaps workers who were killed in an accident of some kind, or maybe they just really liked working there. No one knows for sure, and given the security that surrounds the facility, we most likely never will.

CHAPTER 10
THE BARRIER ISLANDS

S ituated off the Mississippi Gulf Coast at various distances are the barrier islands, namely Ship Island, Cat Island, Horn Island and Petit Bois and one that is no longer there, Caprice Island. It was at one of these, Ship Island, that D'Iberville first landed and established a base camp from which to explore the Gulf Coast mainland. These islands have played a part in the history of the Gulf Coast since that first landing, providing defensive positions during the early days of the Civil War, sanctuary for pirates and privateers and even homes for some of the early settlers. One island, destroyed completely by a hurricane, even provided a place to gamble, complete with ocean-side cabanas. The barrier islands have seen many uses over the years and have many strange tales associated with them, from ghostly pirates to Civil War soldiers still on duty.

SHIP ISLAND

The site of D'Iberville's first landing in the Mississippi Gulf, Ship Island has been a strategic landing and defensive point for settlers and soldiers ever since. The only deep-water harbor between the Mississippi River and Mobile, it saw the flags of France, Spain, England and the United States all flown over its white sand beaches. It also saw the Confederate flag being hoisted over the unfinished Fort Massachusetts before it was abandoned to Union occupation. Later becoming a prison for captured Confederate soldiers, it was guarded by members of the U.S. Second Regiment, otherwise known as the Louisiana Native Guards, one of the first all–African American units. The fort at Ship Island also became a quarantine station in 1880 before the fort closed in 1903, placing the quarantine station on reserve status in 1916. Several lighthouses have served the island over the years, with the first being built in 1853. The last lighthouse, a wooden structure, was burned down by campers in 1972, to be replaced in 1999 with a replica of the burned structure.

When Camille struck the island in 1969, she cut it basically in half, creating East and West Ship Islands. The fort that is on West Ship Island contributed to the development of that island for tourism, while East Ship Island remained in a mostly natural state. It would seem as though the Gulf is slowly reclaiming the island, as Hurricane George in 1998 washed nearly a mile of beach from East Ship Island, and when Katrina struck, she very nearly submerged the entire East Ship Island. West Ship Island saw the most damage, though, with most of the tourist facilities completely wiped out, including the replica lighthouse. Hurricane Ike, which hit Galveston, Texas, in 2008, was most likely responsible for completely submerging the eastern half of the island. By 2009, rebuilding had begun on West Ship Island, with a new visitors' center and facilities being completed and opened for use. Today, you can ride the excursion boat out to West Ship Island and spend the entire day touring the fort and island or simply relaxing on the white sand beaches. But while you're idly strolling along the beach, be sure to watch out for pirates.

Numerous people over the years have reported coming face to face with what some think is Jean Lafitte himself. As the story goes, a man and his wife were walking along the secluded east side of West Ship Island when they suddenly became aware of someone coming up behind them. Thinking it might be another tourist from the excursion boat, they cheerfully turned around to inquire as to how the newcomer liked Ship Island so far. Only it wasn't anyone from this century they faced, but a man dressed in what they described as pirate clothing. The man, sporting a bushy moustache, stopped a few feet from them and demanded to know what they were doing on "his" beach. He then scowled at them before they could reply and disappeared right in front of their eyes. Well, they wasted no time at all in getting back to the excursion boat, preferring to cut their stay a bit short. From the description given, some think that perhaps it was Lafitte protecting the treasure that he supposedly buried on Ship Island from what he considered to be trespassers.

In addition to the pirate on the beach, several people have seen the apparition of a Union soldier walking inside the fort. When approached, he simply fades from sight without interaction of any kind. That's not the case with the fort's resident Confederate soldier though. He appeared suddenly right in front of a lady touring the fort, tipped his hat and then disappeared, the sound of his laughing following the poor lady as she ran from the fort in a complete state of hysterics. Obviously, he found that to be extremely humorous.

HORN ISLAND

Sitting in the Gulf just south of Ocean Springs is Horn Island, with the only structure to speak of being a ranger station. From 1943 to 1945, the U.S. Army took over the island and closed it off to all public use, establishing a biological weapons testing site. It was closed after it was determined that it was too close to populated areas to be effective. Most of the structures built by the army were later destroyed by hurricanes, allowing the island to revert back to its natural state. It was a favorite of Ocean Springs painter Walter Inglis Anderson, who spent much of his time from 1946 to 1965 painting the diverse, ever-changing landscape and the wildlife that called it home. Some think that the ghost that walks the beach of Horn Island is none other than Anderson. Several people have reported seeing the artist walking down the beach carrying the messenger bag containing his paints and canvases. Supposedly, he has even been sighted in the past by rangers at the island, and when approached, he is said to smile and wave at them before disappearing. Anderson was known to camp for several days at a time on Horn Island, which could account for the reports of campfires being spotted on the beach, only to find that when a ranger would investigate the source of the blaze, no traces of a fire would be found. Perhaps Anderson is still visiting the island that he loved spending so much time on, camping next to a spectral fire on the beach.

CAT ISLAND

Once home to Nicholas Christian L'Adnier and later his son-in-law Juan Cuevas, Cat Island has been lived on or otherwise occupied since before 1746. It was used by the U.S. Army in World War II as a site to train dogs;

families would send their pets to the Cat Island War Dog Reception and Training Center, where they would be trained by the Signal Corps. At the time, it was thought that the dogs could be trained to sniff out Japanese Americans because they had a distinctive odor, an experiment that was based on an unsound assumption and was later discarded when it showed no value. The island is unique compared to the other barrier islands in that its beaches are backed up by dense forests of pine and oak and contain bayous and marshes, which are home to alligators and a variety of other animals. The western half and the southern tip of the island are part of the Gulf Islands National Seashore, with the remainder of the island being privately owned; the beach property was purchased by BP as a staging area for cleanup crews working on the 2010 Deepwater Horizon spill.

One of the frequently reported stories associated with this island is that of the soldier. Seen walking the beach area dressed in a World War II green fatigue uniform, he seems to be wandering aimlessly, as if confused or lost. When spotted, he quickly darts into the woods and disappears, and when the area is searched, no one is ever found. Oddly enough for an island that was lived on and utilized as long as this one has been, this is the only story that I could find concerning any hauntings in the area.

CAPRICE ISLAND

Nothing but shallow water marks the spot where Caprice Island once sat; even the freshwater well casing is now gone. Officially called Dog Island or Dog Keys, it was located midway between Horn Island and Ship Island. When the French first arrived, Native Americans told them of an island that would suddenly appear for a number of years and then just disappear, only to appear again at a later date. It was shown on charts in the mid-1800s and was listed as a military reservation. It was known to have disappeared around 1859 and then reappeared around 1890, and by 1930, it had disappeared again—only this time it took some things with it.

With Prohibition in full swing from the 1920s to 1933, a group of three local Biloxi entrepreneurs decided that Dog Island would be the perfect place to set up a casino and bar since it was officially out of the area legally affected by Prohibition. They bought the island with a dream of turning it into the "Monte Carlo of the South" and renamed it the Isle of Caprice. When they purchased the island from the government, it was approximately three and a half miles long and about four hundred yards wide. They immediately built a pier, drilled a freshwater well and constructed beachside cabanas, a dance hall and a casino. They opened the doors on May 30, 1926, telling guests to bring swimsuits and their wallets. Every day, four excursion boats made the trip to the island, and it was a moneymaker from the start. But unfortunately, the island was a mere three feet above sea level and was doomed to a short life. A hurricane hit the island in 1930, wiping out everything and completely submerging the island. Dog Island had once again disappeared into the sea.

Local legend has it that the partiers and gamblers knew that a storm was brewing out in the Gulf but, figuring that it wouldn't be very bad, decided to stay and play on the island instead of evacuating to the relative safety of the mainland. The storm hit and hit hard, and it was two days before rescue boats could be deployed from Biloxi out to gather up the people who had stayed on the island. When they got to the island, all they found were bodies floating in the water amid debris; the island had gone, and no one survived. They say that if you go out where the island used to be, you can hear the sounds of laughter carrying on the wind, suddenly to be replaced with screams and then silence.

The only thing to remain from Caprice was the freshwater well casing that was sticking up out of the ocean, still emitting a stream of fresh water from its depths. As to the validity of this story, well, your guess is as good as mine. I have found several references to it and have had the story told to me in one shape or another by a half dozen people over the years. I have also been told that the businessmen who started the venture closed it down and sold off most of the fixtures when the end of Prohibition put them out of business, all before the hurricane hit that wiped out the island. Either way, I do know several fishermen who won't go out to where the island once sat for any reason at all.

Deer Island

I thought it necessary to include Deer Island—once part of the mainland and not considered to be an actual barrier island—in this section because of one story: the headless pirate. When the island was still attached to the area near Biloxi, it was said that a pirate ship commanded by Captain Pitcher landed on its shores with the intent of burying some treasure; effectively, the pirates intended to empty out their hold and make room for another round

Deer Island near Biloxi. This island used to be part of the mainland and isn't actually a barrier island. They say it houses a headless ghost that protects a buried treasure. *Photo by the author.*

of thievery. After unloading the treasure onto the shore, Captain Pitcher sought out a volunteer to accompany him inland to find a suitable place to bury it. They set out, found just the right spot and made several trips to get the treasure to the burial spot. They dug the hole and buried the treasure, at which point Pitcher drew his sword and ran his helper through. He then decapitated the body and hung the head up in a tree by the hair, thereby reducing the number of people who knew where the treasure was buried to one. He then ran back to the waiting boat, claiming they had been set upon by natives and he had barely escaped with his life.

Several people who have ventured out onto Deer Island have reported seeing the ghost of a headless pirate suddenly appear in front of them with arms outstretched. Scared beyond belief, they have made hasty retreats from the island, leaving the ghost to guard the treasure he lost his head to conceal.

CONCLUSION

The Mississippi Gulf Coast is an area filled with the stories of ghosts and hauntings, with the occasional urban legend thrown into the mix. The residents of the Gulf Coast area seem to be of one camp or the other; they either believe in ghosts or they scoff at the very idea. But with more and more reality shows based on the paranormal cropping up on cable and the increased interest in whether life after death still continues long after the physical body is gone, the camp of the nonbelievers is seeing a marked decrease in its numbers as more and more people are defecting from its ranks over to the believers' side. More and more people, when asked, will readily admit to believing in spirits and demons, and some will even recount their own experiences without much prompting. When people find out that I am a paranormal investigator and writer of collected ghost stories, they suddenly open up with their own experiences, as if looking for validation that they aren't crazy—sort of like going to a priest for confession and absolution. The people of the Gulf Coast are no different, readily sharing their stories with me and pointing me in the direction of someone else that can vouch for their story, all looking for someone to believe them.

That this area has been settled and explored for over three hundred years lends itself well to the birth of ghost stories. The history and times, the turmoil of war and reconstruction all add to the stories passed down through the years, as people recount the experiences that they can find no explanation for, the scary and unexplained encounters that have them questioning their own sanity in some cases.

Conclusion

The haunted history of the Gulf Coast will continue to grow as more paranormal investigators enter the field and make new discoveries, perhaps one day even validating the stories contained within these pages.

BIBLIOGRAPHY

BOOKS

Sillery, Barbara. *The Haunting of Mississippi.* Gretna, LA: Pelican Publishing Company, 2011.

Sullivan, Charles, and Murella Hebert Powell. *The Mississippi Gulf Coast: Portrait of a People.* Northridge CA: Windsor Publications, 1985.

ONLINE SOURCES

Biloxi. Wikipedia. en.wikipedia.org/wiki/Biloxi,_Mississippi.

Biloxi Historical Society. biloxihistoricalsociety.org.

City of Pascagoula. cityofpascagoula.com/history-of-pascagoula.

City of Pass Christian. city.passchristian.net/index.htm.

Gautier. Wikipedia. en.wikipedia.org/wiki/Gautier,_Mississippi.

Bibliography

Gulf and Ship Island Railroad. Wikipedia. en.wikipedia.org/wiki/Gulf_and_Ship_Island_Railroad

Gulfport, Mississippi. Wikipedia. en.wikipedia.org/wiki/Gulfport,_Mississippi.

Horn Island (Mississippi). Wikipedia. en.wikipedia.org/wiki/Horn_Island_%28Mississippi%29.

Long Beach, Mississippi. Wikipedia. en.wikipedia.org/wiki/Long_Beach,_Mississippi.

Long Beach Timeline. Long Beach/Pass Christian. longbeach.passchristian.net/time_line.htm.

Ocean Springs. Wikipedia. en.wikipedia.org/wiki/Ocean_Springs,_Mississippi.

Ocean Springs Archives. www.oceanspringsarchives.net.

Pass Christian, Mississippi. Wikipedia. en.wikipedia.org/wiki/Pass_Christian,_Mississippi.

ABOUT THE AUTHOR

B orn in Lima, Ohio, Bud Steed is the investigation manager for TOPS (The Ozarks Paranormal Society), based in southwest Missouri. A writer and accomplished photographer, Bud writes weekly columns for examiner.com covering the topics of photography, ghosts and ghost hunting and is the author of *The Haunted Natchez Trace*, a book documenting the legends and hauntings of the famous Natchez Trace. A lifelong interest in both the paranormal and history have led him to participate in numerous paranormal investigations, the most notable of these being the investigation at Wilson's Creek National Battlefield, for which TOPS was the first team to receive a permit from the National Park Service to conduct an overnight

investigation of both the battlefield and the historic Ray House. The investigation was filmed by the Travel Channel for its series *Legends of the Ozarks* and produced startling evidence of hauntings at Wilson's Creek.

A firm believer in giving back to his community, Bud enjoys speaking to local elementary school classes about the paranormal, writing and the importance of learning and working hard to achieve their goals. A Freemason belonging to Ash Grove Lodge #100, Bud also participated in the Missouri Child Identification Program (MOCHIP), a free program where parents can receive a computer disk containing all of their children's vital information, including electronic fingerprints and DNA. These disks work in conjunction with any police computer system to aid in Amber Alerts or identification should the child become missing.

Bud has spent much time traveling, including living in Germany and France, as well as touring most of Europe while in the army. He has also lived in nine different states since leaving his home in Ohio in 1979. Bud currently lives near Springfield, Missouri, with his wife, Jennifer, and their four children, David, Sean, Ciara Jo and Kerra.

www.ingramcontent.com/pod-product-compliance
Lightning Source LLC
Chambersburg PA
CBHW060814100426
42813CB00004B/1063